The Great American Microbrewery Beer Book

The Great American Microbrewery Beer Book

Jennifer Trainer Thompson

Photographs by
Kristen Brochmann

Ten Speed Press
Berkeley, California

Text copyright © 1997 by Jennifer Trainer Thompson
Photographs copyright © 1997 by Kristen Brochmann

1☺

Ten Speed Press
P.O. Box 7123
Berkeley, California 94707

Distributed in Australia by E. J. Dwyer Pty. Ltd., in Canada by
Publishers Group West, in New Zealand by Tandem Press, in South
Africa by Real Books, in Singapore and Malaysia by Berkeley Books,
and in the United Kingdom and Europe by Airlift Books.

Cover design by Tracy Dean, Design Site
Interior design by Catherine Jacobes

Library of Congress Cataloging-in-Publication Data

Thompson, Jennifer Trainer.
    The great American microbrewery beer book / Jennifer Trainer
Thompson: photographs by Kristen Brochmann.
        p.   cm.
    Includes bibliographical references and index.
    ISBN 0-89815-818-4
    Beer--United States.   2. Microbreweries--United States.
I. Title.
TP577.T455   1997   96-38121
641.2'3'0973--dc21   CIP

First printing, 1997
Printed in Hong Kong

1 2 3 4 5 6 7 8 9 10 — 01 00 99 98 97

Contents

With special thanks to Glenn Johansson

(D & S Appliances and Television),

Jerry Smith (King's Liquor Store),

Bob West (West's Package),

and Ron Gagon (The Spirit Shop)

on the beer front,

Jody Fijal and Deborah Callan

for their assistance in the kitchen,

Erik Bruun for his good research,

and Brave Dave

for drinking his share.

Introduction

BEER HAS ANCIENT ROOTS. In Mesopotamia, it was drunk as early as 4000 BC. In Ancient Egypt, the Pharaohs assigned a beer inspector to guarantee that beer was brewed to the highest standards. During the age of Confucius, beer was even incorporated into Chinese religious rituals.

Beer arrived in North America with the Pilgrims and the cereal beverage flourished in the colonies with George Washington, Thomas Jefferson, and Samuel Adams all homebrewers of stouts, porters, and other ales. By the mid-1800s, lagers were popular in Germany, Austria, and Czechoslovakia, and waves of immigrants brought recipes to Chicago, St. Louis, Milwaukee, and other American cities. By 1880, there were 2,272 breweries in America—77 in New York City alone! Budweiser was launched in 1876 and became the first mass-market beer.

By the early 1900s, with improved rail transportation, companies such as Anheuser-Busch grew from small regional breweries into large national companies, as many small neighborhood breweries went out of business. The start of prohibition in 1919 was a death knell to small, craft brewers and, by World War II, Americans were drinking flavorless 3.2% alcohol beer and asking for "Buds." By the 1970s, less than 40 breweries existed in America.

As America reached an all-time low in craft brewing, a beer renaissance was occurring in Britain and Europe. Baby boomers on their first trips abroad noticed that beer sold in pubs tasted a lot different from the insipid lagers they were used to. Back in the States, the tide was just starting to turn. Fritz Maytag had purchased the Anchor Brewing Company in the mid-1960s and was trying to restore a local San Francisco beer (steam beer) to its zestful beginnings. The first modern microbrewery—the New Albion Brewing Company in Sonoma, California—opened in 1976 with the brewmaster producing the kinds of English and Scottish ales he'd discovered while stationed abroad. New Albion eventually closed, and was absorbed into the Mendocino Brewing Company, which opened California's first brewpub* in 1983.

---

* A brewpub is a restaurant or brewery where beer is brewed and served. Some brewpubs bottle beers, others serve only draft on the premises. A microbrewery is a brewery that sells beer. This book is a guide to bottled microbrew beers—so it includes brewpubs that bottle beer, as well as microbrewery establishments.

Introduction

In the early 1980s, a few dozen microbreweries sprang up, mostly in California and the Northwest. This fledgling microbrewery movement was fueled by America's quest for fresh food and variety. Today, microbreweries comprise 95% of the 900 plus breweries in the United States. The beer market has reached a plateau overall, yet microbrewery sales (which represent only 2% of the $40 billion American beer market) have been increasing at a rate of nearly 50% per year for the last five years. Industry guru Bill Owens estimates that three new microbreweries open each week. Go into most bars and restaurants and you no longer can ask simply for a beer—you have a mind-boggling choice of stouts, porters, apricot ales, and rauchbiers.

So what exactly is a microbrewed beer? By strict definition, a microbrewery is a brewery that produces 15,000 barrels or less per year. That definition, however, excludes many of the pioneering microbreweries that have enjoyed stunning success in the last decade. In a larger sense, "microbrewed" has come to mean a handcrafted beer made without additives and chemicals. They are fresh, often date stamped, and differ from large domestic brewery beers in that they use no adjuncts. (Commercial beers are brewed with 60-70% malt and adjuncts such as corn or rice, which provide a cheap source of fermentable sugars. As a result, they tend to be lighter in taste, color, and body.) Technically no longer microbreweries because of their size, companies such as the Redhook Brewery and the Boston Beer Company (maker of Sam Adams) are included in this book because of their role in the American microbrewery movement. (Many former microbreweries who no longer can squeeze into the definition are now defining themselves as "craft" brewers.)

For years, the big brewers paid little attention to the microbrewery movement. But when growth takes place only in a small segment of the market, people take note. After years of ignoring the microbrew appeal, the industry giants are introducing so-called microbrews such as Miller's Red Dog and Anheuser-Busch's Red Wolf. (The preponderance of animal names remains a marketing mystery.) They are also buying the competition, reflected in Anheuser-Busch's 20% purchase of Redhook and Miller's purchase of Leinenkugel. Coors is running a television commercial that advertises itself as the only "real" beer, showing a barfly befuddled by the selection of exotics.

Real microbreweries are retaliating with their strongest weapons: great taste, pure ingredients, and well-designed, sometimes funky labels. Many microbrewery beers are voluntarily brewed in accordance with *Reinheitsgebot*, the German Purity Law of 1516, which was written by

Duke Wilhelm IV of Bavaria and decrees that pure beer can include only malt, hops, yeast, and water.

How Beer is Brewed

Flussiges brot—or "liquid bread," as Germans sometimes call beer—is among the world's most elemental beverages. Like wine, it is wonderfully subtle and complex. Brewmasters transform four simple ingredients—malt, water, hops, and yeast—into a remarkable variety of beer styles and tastes.

Malt is to beer what grapes are to wine, giving beer its color, flavor, and body. Malt is made by steeping a grain (usually barley or wheat) in water until it begins to sprout, then drying and roasting the grain to convert its starch to fermentable sugar. The choice of grains and roasting technique greatly affects the flavor and character. (For malt varieties, see page 205.)

The malt is combined with **water,** then heated and mashed. While not a seminal flavor, water can affect beer's taste. Pure water is desired, and geography can play an almost mythical role—the city of Plzen's soft water helps distinguish a pilsner's taste, for example—and many microbrewers believe their local spring or mountain stream water makes for a better brew.

Next, the water and grains are separated, the sweet liquid extracted from the malt is brought to a boil, and **hops** are added for seasoning, aroma, and a dry, herbal bitterness. Hops are cone-shaped flowers that grow on climbing bines, with dozens of varieties grown in vineyards in the American Northwest, the Czech Republic, Germany, Yugoslavia, and England. Hops added at the beginning of the boiling process lend a dry, bitter flavor, while hops added later create an herbal bouquet and fresh "hoppy" finish. (For hop varieties, see page 206.)

The mixture of malt, water, and hops (called the wort) is then cooled, and **yeast** is added to convert the grain's sugar into alcohol. Yeast fermentation occurs in one of two ways, thus dividing the world of beer into two styles: top fermented and bottom fermented.

Top fermentation is the ancient method of brewing, introduced long before refrigeration, where yeast ferments at room temperature and floats to the top of the beer. This produces a malty, complex, sometimes fruity ale, including porters, stouts, and trappist ales. Perhaps not surprisingly, these ales are best served at milder temperatures (never chilled).

Bottom fermentation occurs when the yeast ferments at lower temperatures at the bottom of the beer, a discovery resulting from medieval brewers who found that storing—

or "lagering"—beer in caves at lower temperatures helped stabilize it. Louis Pasteur's seminal discoveries in the mid-1800s about yeast's behavior and pasteurization confirmed these early observations. Lighter, crisper and clearer than ales, lagers include pilsner and oktoberfest, and are generally best enjoyed at colder temperature.

Top Fermented Beers (Ales)

ALTBIER: Originating in the city of Dusseldorf, altbier means "old beer" in German, referring to the way beer was made before the discovery of lager yeast—namely, by fermenting beer with ale yeast and then conditioning it at cold temperatures. Altbiers tend to be yeasty, vinous, well-hopped, and clean tasting—closer to a lager than an ale in taste. Good with cheeses, sausages, and hearty sandwiches.

BARLEY WINE: Assertive, malty, and flamboyantly named, with a rousing taste and spicy bouquet, this is typically a brewer's strongest ale (often with 8% alcohol). Reminiscent of brandy or strong wine, barley wine is often brewed for special occasions. It makes a good nightcap, and should be served cool but not chilled.

BELGIAN ALE: Distinguished by a soft, round mouthfeel, and accentuated by pear notes, this is a strong ale whose light color belies its potent complexity and depth of flavor. Delicious with shellfish or stews, or as an apéritif. Serve at cellar temperature or chilled.

BITTER: Crispy, dry, and often aggressively hopped, this classic English pub beer has a malty aroma and distinctly bitter—almost astringent—aftertaste. Good with burgers and steak and kidney pies. Serve slightly chilled.

BROWN ALE: Similar to pale ale, but darker and sweeter, brown ale has a soft round maltiness and pleasing nuttiness. A sociable beer, good with spicy food, stews, peasant bread, or salads. Serve slightly chilled.

CREAM ALE: A pale, mild, uniquely American ale, cream ale is lagered at cold temperatures or combined with lager.

DRY STOUT: Similar to porter, dry stouts are creamier, darker, and have more bite. With a malty flavor and dry-roasted bitter finish, dry stouts are good with stilton and walnuts, caviar, oysters, or a fine cigar. Serve cool but not chilled.

EXTRA SPECIAL BITTER (ESB): An English style ale with a well-balanced hoppiness and sweet maltiness.

FRAMBOISE: Aromatic, bubbly, and dry, with a delicate raspberry palate, this raspberry lambic is the beer lover's answer to champagne. Delicious with chocolate or raspberry desserts, or in recipes, such as vinaigrettes. Serve at cellar temperature. (See Lambic.)

HEFEWEIZEN: Traditional German hefeweizen (*weizen* is German for "wheat" and *hefe* means "yeast") is fermented with Weihenstephan yeast, giving it a clove and banana bouquet. (See Wheat Beer.)

HOLIDAY ALE: For centuries, brewers have created a strong, spicy iconoclastic ale for the Christmas holidays. Varying from year to year, holiday ale is ideal with Christmas goose, roasted duckling, or roast beef. Serve slightly chilled.

IMPERIAL STOUT: Heavy and complex, an imperial stout is faintly sweet, with notes of coffee and chocolate and a bitterness from the roasted barley. Serve cool but not chilled, with espresso or sharp cheeses.

INDIA PALE ALE (IPA): Born of necessity in the 1700s, this spicy, highly hopped beer was brewed for British colonists stationed in the East Indies. Its high alcohol content enabled it to survive the long sea voyage from England to Calcutta—it's a great beer style, now popular in the hot summer months. Served chilled.

KOLSCH: Kolsch is similar to an altbier, but pale and slightly fruitier. From Cologne, it is still relatively rare in the United States. Serve cool.

KRIEK: A fruity beer made with cherries (*kriek*) and unmalted wheat, and fermented naturally with wild airborne yeast in Belgium's Senne Valley. Sparkling, tart, and freshly sweet with earthy undertones, kriek is good as an apéritif or with sharp cheese, wild game, or desserts. Serve at cellar temperature. (See Lambic.)

LAMBIC: A dry tart beer made with unmalted wheat and malted barley, lambic is fermented naturally with wild airborne yeast in Belgium's Senne Valley. Always aromatic and bubbly, some lambics have a delicately sweet raspberry (*framboise*) palate, while others are made with cherries (*kriek*). Delicious with chocolate or raspberry desserts, or in recipes, such as vinaigrettes. Serve slightly chilled.

OATMEAL STOUT: This is a variation of sweet stout, with oatmeal added for silkiness and flavor. Once prescribed to nursing mothers in Britain, oatmeal stout is tasty with dark breads and heavy cheeses, lobster, steak and kidney pie, and shishkebobs. Serve cool but not chilled.

PALE ALE: Similar to bitter ale, pale ale is drier and cleaner, with a subtle, spicy fruitiness. Named in England when achieving a translucent ale was a novelty, this is an easy, refreshing beer, tasty with Cheddar cheese and apples, chicken pot pie, or seafood. Serve slightly chilled.

PORTER: Complex and intensely flavored with dry coffee overtones and a soft, delicately rounded body, a porter is ideal for those who like a dark beer without the heavy bitter bite of a stout. Indeed, a porter is a good introduction to a stout. American porters tend to be sweeter than British ones. Good with oysters hamburgers, and Cajun foods. Serve cool but not chilled.

SCOTCH ALE: Full-bodied and chewier than English ales, with a rich malty aroma and a faint underlying sweetness, Scotch ale is also known as "wee heavy." Good with burgers, ham and cheese sandwiches, and as a nightcap. Serve slightly chilled.

SPECIALTY ALE: Reminiscent of Belgian fruit beers, these ales are brewed by fermenting beer with unusual ingredients, including pumpkin, chiles, Louisiana rice, and various herbs and spices. Serve slightly chilled.

SWEET STOUT: This is a dark, thick English stout with a beautiful chocolate head and hints of chocolate and coffee. Soft and sweet, this stout is a beer enthusiast's answer to good port—pleasing as an after-dinner drink or midday restorative. Serve cool but not chilled.

TRAPPIST ALE: Brewed by Trappist monks since the Middle Ages, this strong, aromatic and much-revered beer has a soft, fruity, yeasty character and long aftertaste. Good with pâtés, roasts, quesadillas, or chocolates. Serve at cellar temperature. (Only beer brewed at a Trappist monastery can claim to be a "Trappist Ale.")

TRIPEL: The strongest of Trappist Ales. (See Trappist Ale.)

WHEAT BEER: Light and spritzy, with a faint fruitiness and spicy bouquet, wheat beer is brewed with wheat rather than barley and suggests flavors of banana, clove, ginger, and lemon. Traditionally from Bavaria and Belgium, wheat beer is brewed with malted wheat, and is also known as *weisse* (white) or *weizen* (wheat) beer. A thirst-quenching summer drink, popularly garnished with lemon and sometimes a shot of raspberry syrup. Serve slightly chilled to chilled.

WHITE BEER: In Belgium, wheat beer is called *witbier*, or "white beer." Distinct unto itself, white beer is smooth, cloudy, and highly-spiced, with hints of orange and coriander. White beer is brewed with unmalted wheat. An intriguing summer or dessert beer. Serve slightly chilled.

Bottom Fermented Beers (Lagers)

AMBER ALE: This is a general term used to describe copper-colored ales or lagers. Often you'll find amber ales have a medium maltiness and strong hoppy bitterness—fuller bodied, say, than a golden lager. (See Vienna.)

AMERICAN LAGER: Clean, light-bodied, and mild-tasting, American lager is a good summertime beer.

BOCK: This is a strong, malty lager (either dark or light), sometimes with caramel or chocolate undertones, and a fresh, faintly-sweet flavor. Hailing originally from Einbeck, Germany, labels are often decorated with a *bock* or "goat," perhaps inferring the beer's kick. One of the most complex lagers, American versions tend to be lighter flavored. Serve as a winter warmer, or to celebrate spring. Good with spicy foods or grilled lamb. Serve cool or slightly chilled.

CALIFORNIA COMMON BEER: See Steam Beer.

DORTMUNDER: Originally from Dortmund, Germany, this pale lager has more body and less hoppiness than a pilsner. Medium-bodied and slightly fruity, it has a lightly carbonated edge. Also known as an Export beer, serve slightly chilled.

DOUBLE BOCK (DOPPELBOCK): A very strong bock (with twice the alcohol by volume) with an intense malty sweetness balanced by a dry, faintly smoky finish. Often identified by the "ator" suffix, double bocks were originally brewed by monks for Lent, and are still served to celebrate spring's arrival. Good with wild mushrooms, pâtés, and roasted game. Serve cool or slightly chilled.

EXPORT: See Dortmunder.

HELLES: See Munchner.

MAIBOCK: This bock beer is brewed to celebrate the month of May. (See Bock beer.)

MARZENBIER: See Oktoberfest.

MUNCHNER: Also known as a *helles*, or "pale" lager, munchner is a malty, sweet, and drinkable dark beer that originated in Munich in 1928 at the famous Paulaner Brewery.

OKTOBERFEST: Before the days of refrigeration, oktoberfests were brewed with a high alcohol content to preserve them in caves from March through the summer. Malty and faintly sweet, with a fruity roundness and medium body, they were and still are served ceremoniously in the fall at German Oktoberfests. Smooth and quaffable, this lager is good with chowders, pizza, roasted pork, or spicy foods. Serve slightly chilled.

PILSNER: A bright, dry, golden beer originating in Plzen, the Czech Republic, pilsner has a fragrant floral bouquet lent by the late addition of Saaz hops. With lively carbonation, it is best displayed in tall glassware. Good with seafood, garlicky Italian food, or as an apéritif. Serve slightly chilled.

RAUCHBIER: Brewed with malt that has been smoked over a beechwood fire, rauchbier is similar to oktoberfest, but smoother and heavier, with a strong smoky aroma and flavor. It holds its own at barbecues or with smoked sausages, duck, or oysters. Serve cool but not chilled.

STEAM BEER: Originating in the 19th century, steam beer is a highly hopped, medium-bodied foamy beer named for the hissing pressure wooden casks would make when tapped. Using a hybrid fermentation method where lager yeasts are brewed at ale temperatures, steam beers were popular during the Gold Rush and are uniquely American. Anchor Brewing Company (see p. 16) has trademarked the term "Steam Beer"—as a result, this style is called California Common Beer. Serve slightly chilled.

VIENNA: This reddish, somewhat fruity beer was introduced in the 1800s as Vienna's answer to pilsner. Vienna beer is the grandfather of the amber ale that was popular in America at the turn of the century and has been recently revived.

A few beer tips:

- Drinking beer from a glass allows the full flavor and aroma to be released, and the color to be enjoyed. Pour two-thirds of the beer against the side of the glass, then top it off by pouring straight up, letting the natural head perform.

- Many microbrewed beers are made without additives and stabilizers and should be stored in a cool, dark place.

- With the exception of an old ale or barley wine (which mellows like fine wine), beer does not get better with age. It's best when fresh, as the flavor begins to change after one to three months. Check labels for date stamps.

- Beer pairs well with strong flavors—chiles, garlic, and the spices found in Mexican, Italian, Chinese, Thai, African, and Indian dishes.

- Beer should be judged by its appearance, bouquet, taste, body, and after taste, but above all it should be enjoyed. Bread is the staff of life, it is said, but beer is life itself.

Key to Symbols

 Great American Beer Festival gold medal winner

 Great American Beer Festival silver medal winner

 Great American Beer Festival bronze medal winner

 Indicates a beer is brewed in accordance with the German Purity Law.

 Offers tours but often on weekends or by appointment only—call for details before visiting!

 Serves food

Pilsner and *winter seasonal*: Examples of the style or the seasonality of a particular brew.

og: Refers to a beer's original gravity. Based on a British system of 1000 units, an "og of 1.020" means there are 20 units of fermentable matter in 1,000 units water.

abw: Indicates the percentage of alcohol by weight. A low alcoholic beer is 3.5% or less, medium is between 3-6%, and high is 6% or greater. (To convert to alcohol by volume, multiply the number by 1.25.)

NOTE: Missing information indicates that a brewery declined to disclose detailed information about hops, malts, grains, og, and abw out of concern that these details would reveal the formula for a particular beer.

WEST

ALASKA ❦ ARIZONA ❦ CALIFORNIA ❦ COLORADO ❦ MONTANA

NEVADA ❦ OREGON ❦ UTAH ❦ WASHINGTON ❦ WYOMING

Considered ground zero for the American microbrewery beer movement, the West is where the first brewpubs appeared in the early 1980s. The Northwest in particular is known for British-style ales that are brewed with an American twist, taking advantage of locally grown hops from Oregon and Washington. For beer lovers, the West is sheer nirvana: beer is taken as seriously here as chiles are in Texas. (Indeed, when I visited a hotel in Seattle while researching this book, my questions to the hotel porter led to a six-pack of his favorite microbrews being delivered unsolicited to my door that evening.)

ALASKA

Alaskan Brewing Company

Geoff and Marcy Larson started making beer in Juneau in 1986 after painstakingly researching the history of breweries in Alaska before prohibition. Discovering a formula from a defunct gold-rush era brewery, they started with 1,500 barrels of Alaskan Amber that first year. Their steadily growing popularity landed them an appearance on the television series "Northern Exposure," and recently the police had to be called to a Seward pizza joint to calm an irate customer who wouldn't pay for his pizza because he couldn't get Alaskan Amber served along with it. The company is in the midst of a ten-fold facility expansion to be completed in 1998. If you can find it, don't miss their porter smoked with alder. 5429 Shane Dr., Juneau, AK 99801-9540, (907) 780-5866.

Alaskan Amber Beer

(og: 1.057; abw: 4.2%)

Hops: Cascade, Czech Saaz

Malts–grains: Two-row Klages, Pale, Munich

A richly malted, aromatic, amber-colored ale brewed with city water supplied by a glacial ice melt.

Alaskan Pale Ale

(og: 1.048; abw: 3.7%)

Hops: Tettnanger, Willamette, Chinook

Malts/grains: Two-row Klages, Pale, Munich

A light, golden, softly malted ale with a hint of citrus overtones and a crisp, dry finish.

Bottled beers not photographed:

Alaskan Autumn Ale

seasonal

(og: 1.048; abw: 3.4%)

Hops: Cascade, Centennial

Malts/grains: Two-row Klages, Pale, Crystal

Alaskan Smoked Porter

(og: 1.055; abw: 4%)

Hops: Chinook, Willamette

Malts/grains: Two-row Klages, Pale, Chocolate, Black Patent, Crystal

Bird Creek Brewing Company

Founded in 1991 by brewmaster Ike Kelly, Bird Creek is named after Ike's hometown which is nestled along a mountain fjord 25 miles south of Anchorage. The brewery is located in an Anchorage industrial park, and outfitted with converted dairy equipment that gives him a capacity of 5,000 barrels per year. Ike's beers are unpasteurized and unfiltered, using Alaskan glacier water. 310 E. 76th Ave., #B, Anchorage, AK 99518, (907) 344-2473.

Anchorage Ale

(og: 1.045; abw: 5.02%)

Hops: Cascade

Malts/grains: Two-row, Midwestern Barley

With an ample and lasting head, this chestnut-colored ale tastes more like a pale ale, with a perfumed nose that is better than Chanel! If you like hops, you'll love this ale.

Denali Style Ale

(og: 1.045; abw: 5.2%)

Hops: Chinook, Cascade

Malts/grains: Wisconsin Two-row Barley

With a decent head, cloudy rust color, and medium body, this malty, well-balanced brown ale has volumes of taste, with a hint of apples and a crisp hoppy aftertaste. Instead of finishing hops, brewmaster Ike Kelly throws in wildflowers from nearby Denali Park.

Bottled beers not photographed:

Brewed in Alaska Festival Beer

(og: 1.048; abw: 5.2%)

Hops: Saaz

Malts/grains: Two-row, Munich

Iliamna Wheat Raspberry Wheat Beer

(og: 1.044; abw: 5%)

Hops: Saaz

Malts/grains: Wheat, Two-row, Munich

Old 55 Pale Ale

(og: 1.050; abw: 5.3%)

Hops: Chinook, Cascade

Malts/grains: Two-row, Six-row Barley

ARIZONA

Black Mountain Brewing Company

In 1989, Maria and Ed Chilleen opened a microbrewery adjacent to their Satisfied Frog Restaurant in Cave Creek, mostly to keep the restaurant in beer. It was a sleepy operation until Ed came up with the idea of putting a serrano chile instead of a lime into their European-style pilsner— and Cave Creek Chile Beer was born. It took them a year to stabilize the product, and today it's sold worldwide, brewed at both their brewery (which now has a capacity of 108,000 gallons per year) and in Indiana. One distributor in Mexico says his kids beg for the serrano after the beer is drunk. They put the pepper on the table in the hot sun, where the chile heats up and steam from the inside builds up and eventually erupts, causing the chile to shoot across the table. They make other beers, but Chili Beer accounts for "ninety nine and nine tenths percent" of sales, according to brother and general manager Dick Chilleen. 6245 East Cave Creek Rd., Cave Creek, AZ 85331, (800) 228-9742.

Crazy Ed's Original Cave Creek Chili Beer

(og: 1.044; abw: 3.7%)

Hops: Liquid extract hops

Malts/grains: Six-row Barley, plus corn syrup

Oddly enough, the beer is searingly hot (it's like drinking liquid serrano chiles) and the serrano pepper inside is not. A good cooking beer—perfect as a base for steamed mussels.

Bottled beers not photographed:

Crazy Ed's Original Cave Creek Amber

(og: 1.044; abw: 3.7%)

Hops: Liquid hop extract

Malts/grains: Six-row Barley, Black Patent

Crazy Ed's Original Cave Creek Black Mountain Gold

(abw: 4.7%)

Hops: Saaz

Malts/grains: Malted Barley

Crazy Ed's Original Cave Creek Chili Light Beer

(abw: 3.5%)

Hops: Saaz

Malts/grains: Malted Barley

Anchor Brewing Company

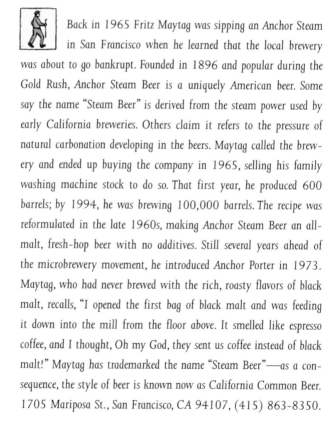

Back in 1965 Fritz Maytag was sipping an *Anchor Steam* in San Francisco when he learned that the local brewery was about to go bankrupt. Founded in 1896 and popular during the Gold Rush, *Anchor Steam Beer* is a uniquely American beer. Some say the name "Steam Beer" is derived from the steam power used by early California breweries. Others claim it refers to the pressure of natural carbonation developing in the beers. Maytag called the brewery and ended up buying the company in 1965, selling his family washing machine stock to do so. That first year, he produced 600 barrels; by 1994, he was brewing 100,000 barrels. The recipe was reformulated in the late 1960s, making *Anchor Steam Beer* an all-malt, fresh-hop beer with no additives. Still several years ahead of the microbrewery movement, he introduced *Anchor Porter* in 1973. Maytag, who had never brewed with the rich, roasty flavors of black malt, recalls, "I opened the first bag of black malt and was feeding it down into the mill from the floor above. It smelled like espresso coffee, and I thought, Oh my God, they sent us coffee instead of black malt!" Maytag has trademarked the name "Steam Beer"—as a consequence, the style of beer is known now as *California Common Beer.* 1705 Mariposa St., San Francisco, CA 94107, (415) 863-8350.

Anchor Steam Beer

Golden retriever red, with a rich, dense head and soft round flavor, this honey-colored beer is naturally carbonated by a German process called *krausening*, in much the same way champagne is carbonated. Medium-bodied, it has a unique flavor that starts out subtly sweet like an ale but vanishes quickly, leaving a hoppiness that lofts to the back of the mouth.

Our Special Ale

seasonal

Anchor has been making a seasonal Christmas ale since 1975, and varies the recipe and label from year to year (the 1995 batch featured a tree, the ancient sign for the winter solstice when the earth with its seasons appears born anew). O.S.A.—as it's known—ages well, and is sold from late November to early January. This year's batch was dark, rich, and syrupy, with a fragrant bouquet reminiscent of nutmeg, vanilla, and anise, and a foresty finish. An early O.S.A. eventually became Liberty Ale.

Anderson Valley Brew Company

Located in *Anderson Valley* (north of San Francisco and the Napa Valley), this funky brewpub in a former saloon was started by chiropractor Kenneth Allen. He bought the building for office space, then realized that the property had one of the best water supplies in Anderson Valley—perfect for brewing beer. Allen now kegs eight styles of beer, plus "whatever the boys cook up." They use no pasteurizing processes, and draw down the water from an 80-foot well out back. The brewery is downstairs, the pub upstairs. 14081 Highway 128, Boonville, CA 95415, (800) 207-BEER.

Anderson Valley Barney Flats Oatmeal Stout

(og: 1.063; abw: 5.09%)

Hops: Eroica, Northern Brewer, Cascade

Malts/grains: Two-row, Munich 20L, Caramel 40L and 80L, Chocolate, Wheat, Roasted Barley, Oats

A rich experience, this stout with its cappuccino-colored foam head is more smooth than sweet, and on the bitter side of bittersweet. There's no sign of chocolate, but the caramel is evident in the taste.

Anderson Valley Belk's Extra Special Bitter Ale

(og: 1.062; abw: 5.7%)

Hops: Eroica, Nugget, Northern Brewer, Mt. Hood

Malts/grains: Two-row Pale, Munich 20L, Caramel 40L

This highly hopped beer has a bitter bite and arousing aromatics. The full bodied quality goes well with spicy dishes.

Anderson Valley Boont Amber Ale

(og: 1.055; abw: 5.079%)

Hops: Eroica, Clusters, Liberty

Malts/grains: Two-row Pale, Caramel 40L and 80L

Voted the best beer in California by the San Francisco Bay Guardian in 1990, this medium bodied, slightly bitter, copper-colored ale has a short-lived head and strong Barley taste. Good with steak, chicken, and other hearty dishes.

Bottled beers not photographed:

Deep Ender's Dark Porter

(og: 1.052; abw: 4%)

Hops: Nugget, Clusters, Liberty

Malts/grains: Two-row Pale, Caramel 40L and 80L, Chocolate

High Roller's Wheat

(og: 1.051; abw: 4%)

Hops: Northern Brewer, Mt. Hood

Malts/grains: Two-row Pale, Wheat

Poleeko Gold

pale ale

(og: 1.052; abw: 4%)

Hops: Eroica, Nugget, Northern Brewer, Cascade

Malts/grains: Two-row Pale, Caramel 40L

Winter Solstice

seasonal

(og: 1.064; abw: 5.4%)

Hops: Northern Brewer, Mt. Hood

Malts/grains: Two-row Pale, Caramel 40L and 80L, Munich 20L, plus cinnamon, vanilla

Belmont Brewing Company

Situated at the foot of Belmont Pier, this Southern California brewpub has great views of the brewery behind the bar, as well as the downtown Long Beach. Brewmaster Malcolm McDonald said he can't satisfy the demand for his top-fermented ales with his small (1,000 barrels per year) tank capacity, and has the bottled beer contract brewed. 25 Thirty-ninth Pl., Long Beach, CA 90803, (310) 433-3891.

Long Beach Crude

(abw: 4.6%)

Hops: Cascade, Mt. Hood

Malts/grains: Two-row Victory, Caramel 90L, Chocolate, Roasted Barley

That's crude as in oil. This dark ruby-colored porter is the brewer's response to Southern Californians' adverse reaction to bitter beer. With a large rich head, this thick-bodied ale has a hoppy bouquet, with coffee undertones and a malty sweetness.

Marathon

(abw: 3.6%)

Hops: Mt. Hood

Malts/grains: Two-row Special Roasted Malts

A golden ale with a foamy head, cloudy color, and light body.

Top Sail

(abw: 4.6%)

Hops: Hallertauer, Mt. Hood

Malts/grains: Two-row Victory, Crystal 90L

With a lavish head, this slightly malty red ale is the color of redwood, with a light body and bitter overtone.

Buffalo Bill's Brewery

You've got to love a guy who makes a beer called "Alimony Ale" and dubs it the bitterest beer in America. Bill Owens is Mr. Beer—he's written manuals on how to open a brewpub, founded several beer magazines and even started a Bill Society where for $10,000 you can become a lifetime member and receive benefits such as a special brew in your honor, a 100-year subscription to his magazine, and spending Christmas eve at Bill's, sitting by the outdoor fireplace (this _is_ California). He's even installed a shrine to Bill at the Buffalo Bill's Brewery (one of America's first brewpubs, which he started in the East Bay in 1983), and encourages visitors to bring fetishes. In 1995 he sold the brewery to Geoff Harries to devote himself to his publications and web site (check out his virtual brewpub at http://www.ambrew.com), but the pub lives on, with beers brewed onsite and contract brewed. 1082 B St., Hayward, CA 94541, (510) 886-9823.

Alimony Ale

(og: 1.072; abw: 7.2%)

Hops: Cascade, Northern Brewer

Malts/grains: Six-row, Crystal, Black Patent

This beer was brewed for Bill's accountant, who was going through a bitter divorce. (The label originally featured a classified advertisement for a new wife.) The hopping rate on this amber ale was tripled from 4 pounds to 12, and its BU (bitterness unit) reached 72 (most American beers are 16 BU). Like his other beers, this amber ale has a gutsy profile and rich, distinctly bitter, hoppy taste. Nothing acrimonious about the flavor though.

Diaper Pail Ale

Hops: Cascade, Northern brewer

Malts/grains: Six-row, Crystal, Black Patent

This one-time ale with its hilarious label was brewed for a bartender who had a baby.

Pumpkin Ale

(og: 1.052; abw: 5.5%)

Hops: Cascade, Northern Brewer

Malts/grains: Six-row, Crystal, Black Patent

Fermented with pumpkin, this slightly bitter ale was inspired by George Washington, a homebrewer who used vegetables in the brewing process. In the fall of 1988, Bill had a six-barrel brewery at his pub and a 40-pound pumpkin in his back yard. He seeded the pumpkin, baked it, then added it to the mash tun along with allspice. The pulp produced starches that were converted to sugars during the mash process, then fermented to make alcohol. Originally a fall seasonal, this beer was so popular that it is now contract brewed at the Dubuque Brewery in Iowa.

Tasmanian Devil

(og: 1.052; abw: 4.4%)

Hops: Southern Brewer, Green Bullet

Malts/grains: Six-row, Wheat, plus demerara sugar

When Bill received a few cans of New Zealand hops in the mail with names like "green bullet," he brewed a beer and was inspired to name it after something from "down under." With a clear, dark-amber color, this mild beer is somewhat bitter, with a musty aroma and smoky clean taste.

Bottled beers not photographed:

Billy Bock

(og: 1.082; abw: 8.4%)

Hops: Cascade, Northern Brewer

Malts/grains: Six-row, Crystal, Black Patent

Golden Pacific Brewing Company

Started in 1981 by a homebrewer, this brewery was originally called One Thousand Oaks, named after a neighborhood in Berkeley. In 1990, it was combined with another small brewery and renamed Golden Pacific Brewing Company, which that year brewed 700 barrels. One of the first micros to brew lagers, it has since branched into ales. By 1995, Golden Pacific was brewing 10,000 barrels, and in 1996 moved into a new brewery on Fourth Street, which gave it the capacity to brew 40,000 barrels per year. 1404 Fourth St., Berkeley, CA 94710, (510) 655-8905.

Golden Gate Original Ale

(og: 1.056; abw: 4.5%)

Hops: Perle, Willamette, Centennial, Tettnanger

Malts/grains: Two-row Pale, Caramel, Chocolate, Munich

An amber ale with a complex malty flavor, suggesting caramel and a touch of roast. Hoppily aromatic, it has a clean bitter finish.

Hibernator Winter Ale 1995

(og: 1.064; abw: 5.13%)

Hops: Perle, Columbus, Kent Goldings

Malts/grains: Two-row Pale, Belgian, Brown

Nutty and smooth, with a big mouth-feel, this hearty, hoppy, ruby-brown ale is made in limited quantities for the winter holidays.

Bottled beers not photographed:

Black Bear Lager

(og: 1.048; abw: 3.4%)

Hops: Perle, Cascade

Malts/grains: Black Patent

Golden Bear Lager

(og: 1.048; abw: 3.7%)

Hops: Tettnanger, Mt. Hood

Malts/grains: Two-row Pale, Wheat, Munich, Carapils, Caramel

Heckler Brewing Company

Founded in 1993 by Keith Hilken, Heckler brews traditional Bavarian lagers. "Life is too short to drink impure beer," claims Hilken, a homebrewer for 12 years, who later served as an apprentice at the Paulaner Brewery in Munich and Das Klein Brauhaus (owned and operated by Prince Luitpold of Bavaria). Available in five states, Hilken's beers are contract brewed by August Schell Brewing Company in New Ulm, Minnesota. "Heckler Brau will never produce any ales, berry beers, honey beers, red beers, or any such foo foo brew house tomfoolery," asserts Hilken. "We are traditionalists to the core." 175 Mackinaw, Tahoe City, CA 96145, (916) 583-2728.

Heckler Brau Hell Lager

(og: 1.050; abw: 4.9%)

Hops: Saaz, Tettnanger

Malts/grains: Two-row Carapils, Caramel, Crystal

A simple Bavarian-style golden pale lager that is medium-hopped, malty and clean, modeled after the "bier" one might find in a small Bavarian brau haus in Munich.

Heckler Brau Oktoberfest

seasonal

(og: 1.054; abw: 6.2%)

Hops: Saaz

Malts/grains: Barley

With a front-of-the-mouth effervescence, this fresh-tasting beer has a full bouquet and sweet spiciness. Good at football games.

Bottled beers not photographed:

Heckler Brau Doppel Bock

(og: 1.072; abw: 5.8%)

Hops: Northern Brewer, Tettnanger

Malts/grains: Two-row Pilsner, Caramel, Munich, Chocolate

J & L Brewing Company

J & L Brewing was formed in San Rafael in 1990 by two home-brewers who commissioned the Golden Pacific Brewing Company in Emeryville to contract-brew and bottle their ales, and TJ's Bar and Grill in Novato to brew draft beers for the restaurant. J & L eventually moved their brewing system to the brewpub adjacent to the restaurant, where they began brewing beer under the name San Rafael Brewing Company. In 1994, the company expanded by adding Cold Spring Brewing Company in Minnesota as an additional contract brewer, and by the end of 1994, Cold Spring was meeting 100% of the bottling requirements. In 1994, they closed their operation at TJ's, sold the equipment to Golden Pacific and negotiated a national sales agreement with Beverage International Group, the parent company of Cold Spring Brewing Company. Corporate office is at 49 Larkspur St., San Rafael, CA 94901, (415) 457-2842.

San Rafael Amber Ale

(og: 1.060; abw: 4%)

Hops: Bullion, Cascade, Willamette, Tettnanger

Malts/grains: Two-row Pale, Munich, Crystal 60-80L, Crystal 90-110L, Crystal 135-155L

A medium-bodied amber with a caramel maltiness that yields a smooth mouth-feel and well balanced beer.

CALIFORNIA

San Rafael Golden Ale

(og: 1.054; abw: 3.5%)

Hops: Cascade, Tettnanger

Malts/grains: Two-row Pale, Raw Rolled Wheat

A clean, flowery, fruity tasting ale that is welcome in warm weather.

San Rafael Red Diamond Ale

(og: 1.050; abw: 3.75%)

Hops: Bullion, Cascade, Willamette, Tettnanger

Malts/grains: Two-row Pale, Munich, Crystal 60-80L, Crystal 90-110L,Crystal 135-155L, Raw Rolled Wheat

Light red in color, this soft uncomplicated ale has a light sweet taste and mild aroma.

Karl Strauss' Old Columbia Brewery

 Karl Strauss' main brewery facility is located near the San Diego Sports Arena, where Karl Strauss Amber Lager is bottled and kegged for distribution to several hundred restaurants in the San Diego area. You can also visit Karl Strauss' Old Columbia Brewery downtown (San Diego's first microbrewery in 50 years), which serves hearty food and ten Karl Strauss beers on tap. (Draft beers are also available in one-gallon jugs.) Master brewer Karl Strauss, who has received both the Master Brewers Association of the Americas' Award of Honor and Award of Merit, was raised at his father's brewery in Minden, Germany, and spent 44 years as vice president of production at Pabst. 1157 & 1167 Columbia St., San Diego, CA 92101, (619) 234-2739. (A second brew-pub, Karl Strauss Brewery Garden, is located at 9675 Scranton Road in San Diego.)

Karl Strauss Amber Lager

(og: 1.050; abw: 4%)

Malts/grains: Domestic Two-row Caramel

A simple beer reminiscent of mild Bavarian dark beers, with a touch of spiciness.

Lost Coast Brewery and Cafe

You'll find this brewpub in a turn-of-the-century building on the edge of Old Town (the bottling plant is just down the street). Founded in 1990 by two women, the pub features spicy foods as well as darts, pinball, pool, and an annual Octoberfest. 617 Fourth St., Eureka, CA 95501, (707) 445-4480.

Alleycat Amber Ale

(og: 1.050; abw: 3.92%)

Hops: Mt. Hood, Liberty, Cascade

Malts/grains: Carapils, Crystal

With a pretty amber hue, this medium-bodied ale has a mild aroma and a muted hoppy flavor.

Downtown Brown

(og: 1.050; abw: 4%)

Hops: Chinook, Cascade, Mt. Hood

Malts/grains: Roasted Barley, Chocolate

This auburn-colored beer with its persistent lacy head has a strong cascade hop aroma accompanied by a wispy malty taste.

Mad River Brewing Company

Located northeast of Eureka in Northern California, Mad River was founded in 1989 by Bob Smith, an award-winning homebrewer (and former employee of Sierra Nevada Brewing Company) who fulfilled a life dream in opening this company. The name is derived from a local river, which is also the source of the brewery's water supply. The company makes handcrafted ales in a 17-barrel British-style brewhouse. 195 Taylor Way, Blue Lake, CA 95525, (707) 668-4151.

Jamaica Brand Red Ale

(og: 1.065; abw: 3.84%)

Hops: Clusters, Cascade, Willamette, Chinook

Malts/grains: Pale, Medium Crystal, Dark Crystal

Crisp and hoppy with a citrus-spice aroma, this medium-bitter, full-bodied ale is robust and slightly malty.

Steelhead Extra Pale Ale

(og: 1.054; abw: 3.2%)

Hops: Clusters, Cascade, Tettnanger, Willamette, Chinook

Malts/grains: Pale

Mad River's flagship beer, this bright, dry, golden-hued ale starts off fruity and smooth, followed by a sharp hop bitterness and crisp finish.

Bottled beers not photographed:

Steelhead Extra Stout

(og: 1.071)

Hops: Clusters, Cascade, Willamette

Malts/grains: Pale, Medium Crystal, Dark Crystal, Chocolate, Roasted Black Patent

CALIFORNIA

Mendocino Brewing Company

When America's first microbrewery (the New Albion Brewing Company in Sonoma) closed its doors in the early 1980s, the equipment was purchased by Mendocino Brewing Company, who opened California's first brewpub in 1982. A favorite among beer lovers, Mendocino is located in a 19th-century brick building that once housed the Hop Vine Saloon. (A hundred miles north of San Francisco, on the main route to Mendocino, Hopland was once a rich hop-growing area until a hop vine blight devastated the area in the 1950s.) Named after local birds and sporting beautiful labels, all beers are bottle-conditioned (fermented in the bottle) so you'll find a layer of brewer's yeast on the bottom of the bottle. Keep the beer upright, don't shake it, and pour slowly. According to Celebrator Beer News, the company went public in 1994 to build a new $12 million brewery in Ukiah. 13351 Highway 101 S., Hopland, CA 95449, (707) 744-1015.

Blue Heron Ale

(abw: 5.25%)

Hops: Clusters, Cascade

Malts/grains: Pale

First brewed as a spring seasonal in 1985, this India Pale Ale is named after the Great Blue Herons that nest near Hopland along the Russian River. Golden and slightly hazy, it has a deliciously sharp, bitter flavor from the predominance of hops—appreciated in hot weather.

Red Tail Ale

Hops: Clusters, Cascade

Malts/grains: Two-row Barley, Pale, Caramel

A direct descendant of the New Albion Brewing Company, Red Tail is fermented using the same strain of brewer's yeast (indeed, New Albion hop vines grow in the beer garden behind the brewery). The flagship of the Mendocino Brewery, this hoppy amber ale is well-balanced, with a nutty maltiness and herbal finish.

Bottled beers not photographed:

Black Hawk Stout

(abw: 4.5%)

Hops: Cascade, Clusters

Malts/grains: Black Patent, Pale, Caramel

Frolic Shipwreck Scottish Ale

Hops: Goldings, Fuggles

Malts/grains: Caramel, Carastan

The Eye of the Hawk Strong Ale

Malts/grains: Pale, Caramel

Yuletide Porter

winter seasonal

Hops: Clusters, Cascade

Malts/grains: Pale, Caramel, Black Patent

North Coast Brewing Company

While living in England in the 1970s, Mark Ruedrich became interested in "real beer" and the Campaign for Real Ale (a consumer-led English campaign begun in 1971 to bring back cask-conditioned ales). Homebrewing back in Northern California, Ruedrich met Tom Allen and Joe Rosenthal at Fort Bragg, a coastal town along the rugged coast north of San Francisco. Teaming up to start a brewery, they found a Victorian building (that had seen previous life as both a mortuary and a church), which in 1988 they reincarnated as the North Coast Brewing Company Tap Room and Grill. A new facility was opened in 1995, expanding production to 15,000 barrels per year. 444 N. Main St., Ft. Bragg, CA 95437, (707) 964-2739.

Old No. 38 Stout

(og: 1.056; abw: 4.3%)

Hops: Yakima Valley

Fashioned in the style of Dublin Dry Stout and named for a steam engine retired from the Fort Bragg to Willits run, this malty ale is milky and smooth, with the toasted character and coffee notes of dark malts and roasted Barley. Try it with chocolate.

CALIFORNIA

Ruedrich's Red Seal Ale

(og: 1.057; abw: 4.2%)

Hops: Yakima Valley

Malts/grains: Two-row Barley

Amber colored with a slight cloudiness, this light-tasting pale ale has a perfumed floral aroma and soft effervescent taste. Good with grilled meats.

Bottled beers not photographed:

Blue Star Wheat Beer

(og: 1.047; abw: 3.8%)

Hops: Noble
Malts/grains: Malted Wheat, Barley

Schrimshaw Pilsner Style Beer

(og: 1.045)

Hops: Hallertauer, Tettnanger
Malts/grains: Munich, Klages

Pete's Brewing Company

While essentially a contract beer produced in Minnesota, Pete's Brewing Company has done much to further awareness of hand-crafted beers, and Pete's Wicked is recognized as a good, preservative-free commercial alternative to Budweiser et al. In 1979, Pete Slosberg began homebrewing after a futile attempt at making homemade wine. A Silicon Valley computer programmer, he began brewing commercially in 1986, shipping 10,000 cases of beer with his white bull terrier Millie on the label. He soon got a bullying letter from Anheuser-Busch telling him to drop the dog, which competed with their Spuds McKenzie. Not one to bark at the competition, he rethought the label, introduced 22-ounce bottles to the market in 1990, and experienced sales growth of 2,558% from 1989 to 1993. (Sales in 1994 were $33 million, which prompted Inc. Magazine to recognize Pete's Brewing Company as the 79th fastest growing private company in America.) "The Pete," as his wife calls him, brewed 354,000 barrels of Pete's Wicked Ale last year and is hoping to use some of his money from a 1995 public offering to build a $30 million brewery in Northern California. Meanwhile, corporate headquarters are at 514 High St., Palo Alto, CA 94301, (415) 328-7383.

Pete's Wicked Ale

(og: 1.052; abw: 4.2%)

Hops: Cascade, Brewer's Gold

Malts/grains: Pale, Caramel, Roasted Chocolate

Brewed in the tradition of a classic brown ale, this deep amber-colored ale is a good commercial beer, with a floral hop aroma, slightly bitter-sweet flavor, and sharp astringent taste.

Pete's Wicked Winter Brew

winter seasonal

(og: 1.052; abw: 4.1%)

Hops: Cascade, Tettnanger, Liberty

Malts/grains: Pale, Caramel, plus raspberry, nutmeg

This full-bodied, fragrant holiday amber ale has a good mouth-feel, and lacy veil of foam that clings to the side of the glass. The 1995 brew featured a recipe by Walter Do-browney, the 1993 National Homebrew Grand Champion.

Bottled beers not photographed:

Pete's Wicked Amber Ale

(og: 1.050: abw: 3.85%)

Hops: Tettnanger, Yakima Clusters, Cascade

Malts/grains: Munich, Pale, Caramel

Pete's Wicked Honey Wheat

(og: 1.051; abw: 3.8%)

Hops: Tettnanger, Cascade

Malts/grains: Pale, Wheat, Caramel, plus clover honey

Pete's Wicked Bohemian Pilsner

(og: 1.048; abw: 3.9%)

Hops: Tettnanger, Saaz, Yakima Clusters

Malts/grains: Pale, Caramel

Pete's Wicked Maple Porter

(og: 1.055; abw: 4%)

Hops: Yakima Clusters, Yakima Tettnanger, Mt. Hood

Malts/grains: Caramel, Chocolate, Pale, plus maple syrup

Pete's Wicked Multi Grain

(og: 1.055; abw: 3.85%)

Hops: Yakima Clusters, Cascade

Malts/grains: Wheat, Caramel, Barley, Rye, Oats

Pete's Wicked Pale Ale

(og: 1.055; abw: 4%)

Hops: Cascade, Yakima Clusters, Saaz

Malts/grains: Pale, Wheat

Pete's Wicked Strawberry Blonde

(og: 1.050; abw: 3.7%)

Hops: Yakima Clusters, Yakima Tettnanger

Malts/grains: Pale, Wheat, plus natural strawberry flavoring

Pete's Wicked Summer Brew

seasonal

(og: 1.048; abw: 3.9%)

Hops: Tettnanger

Malts/grains: Pale, Wheat

San Andreas Brewing Company

About 45 minutes east of Monterey, the San Andreas Brewing Company opened in 1988 in earthquake country (Hollister sits atop several geological fault lines and has proved inspiration for many of the company's beers). The brewery produces four flagship beers as well as seasonal draft beers, including an apricot ale made with fresh local Blenheim apricots, not to mention Survivor Stout, which was introduced after the 1989 earthquake. If by chance you visit during an earthquake, brewmaster Bill Millar will serve you nickel drafts. 737 San Benito St., Hollister, CA 95023, (408) 637-7074.

Earthquake Porter

Hops: Chinook, Clusters, Goldings

Malts/grains: Two-row Pale, Crystal, Chocolate, Roasted Barley

With a decent head, this interesting espresso-colored porter has a hearty body, with the soft chocolate and coffee complexities courtesy of the roasted malts. It concludes with a hoppy finish and the lingering aroma of smoky coffee.

Oktoberquake

fall seasonal

I couldn't find fault with this honey-colored lager—with a rich, creamy head, it's a clean, well-balanced brew with nutty undertones, and a soft aftertaste suggestive of honey.

Seismic Ale

Hops: Cascade, Chinook, Clusters, Goldings

Malts/grains: Crystal, Munich

With a head that's quicker than the eye, this honey-colored ale has hoppy overtones, with a slight bitter finish and pronounced fruitiness reminiscent of a lambic.

Bottled beers not photographed:

Earthquake Pale Ale

Hops: Cascade, Chinook, Tettnanger

Malts/Grains: Crystal

Kit Fox Amber

Hops: Chinook, Clusters, Cascade, Goldings

Malts/grains: Crystal, Munich

Survivor Stout

seasonal

Hops: Chinook, Goldings, Clusters

Malts/grains: Chocolate, Roasted Barley

San Francisco Brewing Company

Living on Telegraph Hill, homebrewer Allan G. Paul loved stories about San Francisco's wild and woolly days when the gold-fevered forty-niners hung out at saloons in this Barbary Coast neighborhood. Only one bar remains from those days, and it reeks of history—it's where Baby Face Nelson was captured by the FBI and boxing champ Jack Dempsey worked as a bouncer. The bar survived prohibition by serving clams and oysters (and alcohol purely for medicinal purposes) and in 1985 Paul restored the 1907 saloon as the San Francisco Brewing Company. It's a casual place where you can play darts, chess, and backgammon, and sample his unbelievably fresh beer, which is bottled by hand in 200-gallon batches. (Allan brews only 1,000 barrels per year.) 155 Columbus Ave., San Francisco, CA 94133, (415) 434-3344.

San Francisco Brewing Company Albatross Lager

(og: 1.046)

Hops: Hallertauer, Saaz

Malts/grains: Klages, Caramel

This classic Czech-style pilsner has a spicy hop aroma, light malt taste, and effervescent flavor. The color of amber rays, this cloudy unfiltered lager is as fresh as they come, with more taste than you'd expect given its light color.

San Francisco Brewing Company Shanghai IPA

(og: 1.061)

Hops: Kent Goldings, Cascade, Chinook

Malts/grains: Klages, Caramel

This cloudy IPA begs for a hot climate, teasing you with its ribbons of fruitiness and yeasty hoppiness.

Bottled beers not photographed:

Andromeda Wheat

(og: 1.040)

Hops: Saaz, Hallertauer

Malts/grains: Klages, Wheat

Emperor Norton Lager

marzen beer

(og: 1.056)

Hops: Saaz

Malts/grains: Klages, Munich, Caramel, Carapils

Gripman's Porter

(og: 1.062)

Hops: Cascade

Malts/grains: Klages, Caramel

Pony Express Amber Ale

(og: 1.043)

Hops: Cascade

Malts/grains: Klages, Caramel, Carapils

Santa Cruz Brewing Company

This brewpub in downtown Santa Cruz recently celebrated its tenth anniversary. You can watch the beer brewing while you eat, and enjoy the 13 Santa Cruz brews on tap. 516 Front St., Santa Cruz, CA 95060, (408) 429-8838.

Lighthouse Amber

(abw: 3.8%)

Hops: Northern Brewer, Chinook, Hallertauer, Tettnanger

Malts/grains: Pale, Caramel

A smooth, quaffable amber, with a pronounced hop bitterness.

Lighthouse Lager

(abw: 3.8%)

Hops: Clusters, Hallertauer

Malts/grains: Pale

A tasty beer dense with flavor and a lasting finish.

Sierra Nevada Brewing Company

 One of the earliest microbreweries, Sierra Nevada is a great success story. The brewery was started in 1981 by two homebrewers who spent two years building it in their spare time with equipment adapted from dairy parts and scrap metals. With folks on Compuserve raving that Sierra Nevada is "possibly the best beer in America," founders Ken Grossman and Paul Camusi pride themselves on using only the whole cone hop, never hop extracts or pellets. Also, a large portion of hops is added late in the boil so volatile oils are retained, which adds to the aroma of the beers. Growing at a rate of 50% annually, they moved to a new brewing facility in 1989, which gave them the capacity for 200,000 barrels per year, and allowed them to open an adjacent taproom and restaurant. 1075 E. 20th St., Chico, CA 95928, (916) 893-3520.

Sierra Nevada Pale Ale

(og: 1.052; abw: 4.4%)

Hops: Perle, Cascade

Malts/grains: Two-row Barley, Caramel, plus dextrin

This dry crisp ale is classically Cascade-hopped, with much clarity, a fragrant bouquet, and pungent spiciness.

Sierra Nevada Porter

(og: 1.058; abw: 4.7%)

Hops: Nugget, Willamette

Malts/grains: Two-row Barley, Caramel, Chocolate, Black Patent, plus dextrin

Proclaimed "the best (porter) brewed anywhere in the world" by Michael Jackson (the other Michael Jackson), this dark porter has a creamy lasting head, plenty of body, and a malty smooth finish that leaves you deeply satisfied.

Bottled beers not photographed:

Sierra Nevada Bigfoot Barleywine Style Ale

winter seasonal

(og: 1.092; abw: 10.1%)

Hops: Nugget, Cascade, Centennial

Malts/grains: Two-row Barley, Caramel

Sierra Nevada Celebration Ale

holiday seasonal

(og: 1.064; abw: 5.1%)

Hops: Chinook, Cascade, Centennial

Malts/grains: Two-row Barley, Caramel, plus dextrin

Sierra Nevada Pale Bock

spring seasonal

(og: 1.064; abw: 5.2%)

Hops: Perle, Mt. Hood

Malts/grains: Two-row Barley, plus dextrin

Sierra Nevada Stout

(og: 1.064; abw: 4.8%)

Hops: Chinook, Cascade

Malts/grains: Two-row Barley, Caramel, Black Patent, plus dextrin

Sierra Nevada Summerfest

seasonal pilsner

(og: 1.046; abw: 3.5%)

Hops: Perle, Hallertauer

Malts/grains: Two-row Barley, plus dextrin

SLO Brewing Company

San Luis Obispo's first brewpub since prohibition, SLO Brewing was started by brewmaster and president Michael Hoffman, an award-winning winemaker who found beer more fun and less pretentious, and dry hops all his beers. The brewpub is located in an historic hardware building in downtown San Luis Obispo, and Hoffman offers $1 beers and free appetizers during Monday night football. Bottled beers are contract-brewed by August Schell Brewing Company. 119 Garden St., San Luis Obispo, CA 93401, (805) 543-1843.

Brickhouse Extra Pale Ale

(og: 1.045; abw: 4%)

Hops: Nugget, Northern Brewer, Willamette

Malts/grains: Two-row, Munich, Crystal 10L

Lightly cloudy, this pleasant ale is almost firm tasting, with a pleasant hoppy flavor.

Garden Alley Amber Ale

(og: 1.056; abw: 5%)

Hops: Centennial, Nugget

Malts/grains: Two-row, Crystal 10L, Crystal 50-60L, Crystal 95-115L

The brewpub's flagship, this is a smooth and easy amber ale with a fragrant hop aroma and light finish.

Bottled beers not photographed:

Cole Porter

(og: 1.064; abw: 5%)

Hops: Nugget, Willamette

Malts/grains: Two-row, Munich, Crystal 50-60L, Crystal 95-115L, Chocolate, Black Patent, Roasted Barley

Holidaze Ale

winter seasonal

(og: 1.050; abw: 5%)

Hops: Nugget, Centennial

Malts/grains: Two-row, Munich, Crystal 50-60L, Crystal 95-115L, Roasted Barley, plus herbs

Sudwerk Privatbrauerei Hübsch

 Founded in 1990, this large brewpub with its cheerful beer garden brews lagers in the traditional Bavarian style. Sudwerk is located in the Central Valley (between the Sierra Nevada Mountains and California's Coastal region) in the city of Davis, home to UC Davis and 22,000 students. All Hübsch beers are unpasteurized and should be consumed within 90 days. Just blocks from the Davis Amtrak station, Sudwerk was recently named the best "watering hole" by the Sacramento branch of the California Restaurant Association. (Don't miss the french fries!) 2001 Second St., Davis, CA 95616, (916) 758-8700.

Hübsch Lager

(og: 1.047; abw: 3.9%)

Hops: Hallertauer, Perle, Tettnanger

Malts/grains: Two-row, Crystal, Munich, Carapils

A clear, golden, evenly-balanced lager with a light taste and restrained malty flavor.

Hübsch Marzen

(og: 1.053; abw: 4.5%)

Hops: Hallertauer, Perle, Tettnanger

Malts/grains: Two-row, Crystal 20-30L, Munich, Carapils, Crystal 40-70L

Brewed in the oktoberfest style, this uncomplicated amber lager has a smooth soft finish.

Bottled beers not photographed:

Hübsch Doppel Bock

winter seasonal

(og: 1.074)

Hops: Hallertauer

Malts/grains: Chocolate

Hübsch Hefe Weizen

(og: 1.050)

Hübsch Mai Bock

spring seasonal

(og: 1.066)

Hops: Tettnanger

Hübsch Pilsner

(og: 1.050)

Hops: Hallertauer, Perle, Tettnanger

Malts/grains: Pale, Two-row

William & Scott Brewing Company

This beer dates back to the early 1990s, when marketing executive Scott Griffiths sponsored a softball team and decided to serve them his own beer. The players liked it so much that he put it in a local restaurant, and Rhino Chaser American Amber Ale was born. The company now distributes nationally, and has a Rhino Chasers Brewpub at the Los Angeles International Airport. The name "rhino chaser" derives from the Pacific surfers of the 1960s who used "guns" (surfboards) to search the world for the biggest waves—the giant 40-foot "rhinos." The label inspired so much grief from wildlife groups (as if drinking beer would make you want to shoot a rhino) that they donate some of their profits to wildlife conservation projects. Beers are contract brewed in Utica, New York. Corporate office located at 2130 Main St., Huntington Beach, CA 92648, (714) 374-3222.

Rhino Chasers American Amber Ale

(1.050; abw: 4%)

Hops: Fuggles, Mt. Hood, Cascade, Willamette

Malts/grains: Pale, Caramel

A crisp brew with full malt and hop flavor. This flagship beer has devoted fans, though some claim the beer isn't as good as it once was now that's contract brewed.

Bottled beers not photographed:

Rhino Chasers Dark Roasted Lager

(og: 1.051; abw: 4%)

Hops: Clusters, Perle, Saaz, Mt. Hood

Malts/grains: Pale, Black Patent, Caramel, Carapils

Rhino Chasers Peach Honey Wheat

(og: 1.049; abw: 3.7%)

Hops: Tettnanger, Mt. Hood, Clusters

Malts/grains: Roasted Wheat, Pale, Munich

Rhino Chasers Winterful

winter seasonal

(og: 1.052; abw: 4.35%)

Hops: Yakima, Cascade, Liberty

Malts/grains: Pale, Carapils, Caramel, Black Patent

COLORADO

Champion Brewing Company

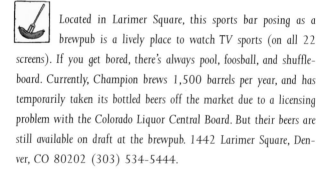

Located in Larimer Square, this sports bar posing as a brewpub is a lively place to watch TV sports (on all 22 screens). If you get bored, there's always pool, foosball, and shuffleboard. Currently, Champion brews 1,500 barrels per year, and has temporarily taken its bottled beers off the market due to a licensing problem with the Colorado Liquor Central Board. But their beers are still available on draft at the brewpub. 1442 Larimer Square, Denver, CO 80202 (303) 534-5444.

Home Run Ale

(og: 1.054; abw: 5%)

Hops: Nugget, Cascade, Willamette

Malts/grains: Chocolate, Roasted Barley

A nondescript filtered beer that's thirst-quenching while watching the games.

Norm Clarke Sports Ale

(og: 1.048; abw: 4.5%)

Hops: Tettnanger, Hersbrucker, Spalt

Malts/grains: English Two-row, Carapils, Caramel, Wheat, Munich

A light-bodied extra pale ale specialty formulated for a local sportswriter who apparently had some dirt on the brewmaster.

Bottled beers not photographed:

Larimer Red

(og: 1.059)

Hops: Centennial, Cascade

Malts/grains: Munich, Vienna, Caramel, Carapils, Roasted Barley

Crested Butte Brewery & Pub

 Nine thousand feet above sea level on the western slope of the Rockies, Crested Butte is the wildflower capital of Colorado, as well as the home of the Mountain Bike Hall of Fame. Popular with skiers, this tiny (1,000 barrel) brewpub began in 1991. Bottled beers are contract brewed by Broadway Brewing Company in Denver. 226 Elk Ave., Crested Butte, CO 81224, (303) 349-5026.

Red Lady Ale

(og: 1.050; abw: 3.99%)

Hops: Chinook, Perle, Tettnanger, Willamette

Malts/grains: Pale, Caramel, Chocolate

Named after Red Lady Mountain, this English-style bitter is the Crested Butte flagship. With a long-lasting head, it's soft and light, with a clean bitter finish.

White Buffalo Peace Ale

(og: 1.050; abw: 4.07%)

Hops: Perle, Oregon Fuggles, Cascade

Malts/grains: Pale, Munich, Caramel, Chocolate

This American-style pale ale is rather still, with a subdued flavor and hop bite.

Bottled beers not photographed:

Buck's Wheat

(og: 1.048; abw: 3.86%)

Hops: Hallertauer, Czech Saaz

Malts/grains: Pale, Wheat

India Pale Ale

(og: 1.056; abw: 4.62%)

Hops: Cascade, Willamette, Fuggles, Saaz

Malts/grains: Pale, Munich, Caramel

Rodeo Stout

(og: 1.052; abw: 3.57%)

Hops: Chinook, Perle

Malts/grains: Pale, Caramel, Oats, Roasted Barley, Black Malt Flour, Chocolate

Three-Pin Grin Porter

(og: 1.049; abw: 3.69%)

Hops: Perle, Fuggles, Saaz

Malts/grains: Pale, Caramel, Chocolate, Roasted Barley

Flying Dog Brewpub

 Two blocks from the gondola, this brewpub was Aspen's first brewery in 100 years. The brewpub brews 27 draft styles (everything from wheat to Russian Imperial Stout), and recently opened Broadway Brewing Company to bottle Flying Dog. The pub, which specializes in locally raised limousin beef, has outdoor dining, and live bluegrass in the summer. 424 E. Cooper St., Aspen, CO 81602, (970) 925-2672.

Flying Dog Doggie Style Ale

(og: 1.048; abw: 5.1%)

Hops: Yakima Chinook, Yakima Cascade

Malts/grains: Pale, Caramel

A deliciously fruity, hoppy IPA.

H. C. Berger Brewing Company

Opened in 1992 in an industrial park near the airport, this brewery is named after brewmaster Sandy Jones' homebrewing grandfather. The first beer invited to the Aspen Food & Wine Festival, the company was recently bought by Peter and Bob Davidoff, native Coloradans whose grandfather owned Tavern on the Green in New York City. A recent expansion allowed capacity to leap from 5,000 to 20,000 barrels per year. 1900 E. Lincoln Ave., Fort Collins, CO 80524, (970) 493-9044.

H. C. Berger Chocolate Stout

Malts/grains: Dry Roasted English Dark, Chocolate

Thin for a stout, this ale has a sweet-smoky aroma, and smoky malt profile with hints of chocolate and peat.

COLORADO

H. C. Berger Indego Pale Ale

Hops: Clusters, Tettnanger, Hersbrucker

Malts/grains: Black Patent, Roasted Barley, Vienna, Wheat, Two-Row

This amber-colored ale is a little roasty, with an interesting malty nose.

Red Raspberry Wheat Ale

Malt/Grains: Wheat, Two-Row, Crystal, plus red raspberries

Brewed with 50% malted wheat and fresh red raspberries, this hazy golden-red ale is tangy and fruity, with a wheaty flavor and sweet raspberry taste and bouquet.

Bottled beers not photographed:

Colorado Golden Ale

Hops: Cascade, Willamette, Perle

H. C. Berger Dunkel

Hops: Spalt, Hersbrucker

Malts/grains: Two-Row, Wheat, Munich, Vienna

H. C. Berger Kolsch

Hops: Cascade, Perle, Willamette

Malts/grains: Wheat, Crystal, Pale

Red Banshee Ale

Hops: Clusters, Chinook, Tettnanger

Malts/grains: Pale, Crystal, Roasted Barley

Whistlepin Wheat Ale

Hops: Cascade, Perle

Malts/grains: Wheat, Pale

High Point Brewing

Incorporated in 1994, High Point is owned by three college buddies with a passion for beer. Their beer is contract-brewed by Lonetree, though they are hoping to build their own facility in 1997. Last year they brewed 1,500 barrels, selling mostly in Colorado, but also Arkansas, Arizona, and Wyoming. Corporate office: 4910 Fox St., Unit E, Denver, CO 80216, (303) 297-8568.

High Point ESB Ale

(og: 1.062; abw: 7%)

Hops: Columbia, Centennial, Cascade, Willamette, Hallertauer

Malts/grains: Two-row, Caramel

This cross-dresser has the astringent hoppiness of an IPA along with the residual maltiness of an ESB.

Lonetree Brewing

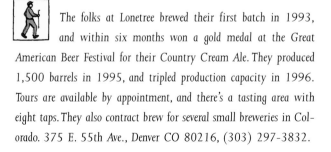

The folks at Lonetree brewed their first batch in 1993, and within six months won a gold medal at the Great American Beer Festival for their Country Cream Ale. They produced 1,500 barrels in 1995, and tripled production capacity in 1996. Tours are available by appointment, and there's a tasting area with eight taps. They also contract brew for several small breweries in Colorado. 375 E. 55th Ave., Denver CO 80216, (303) 297-3832.

Lonetree Iron Horse Dark Ale

(og: 1.064; abw: 7.4%)

Hops: Perle, Willamette

Malts/grains: Roasted Barley, Chocolate

Brewed with dark roasted grains and hops to produce a rich, full-bodied flavor, this ale is enjoyed by many who say they don't like dark beer.

Bottled beers not photographed:

Country Cream Ale

(og: 1.050; abw: 4.6%)

Hops: Mt. Hood, Northern Brewer, Hallertauer

Malts/grains: Six-row, Crystal Barley, Wheat

Horizon Honey Ale

(og: 1.052; abw: 5.7%)

Hops: Cascade

Malts/grains: Two-row, Caramel, plus Colorado honey

Sunset Red Ale

(og: 1.054; abw: 4.64%)

Hops: Northern Brewer, Tettnanger, Hallertauer

Malts/grains: Caramel, Six-row

New Belgium Brewing Company

Not only does New Belgium have some of the most creative labels in the business, this microbrewery also brews exceptional Belgian-style Trappist ales. Founded in 1991 by basement homebrewers Jeffrey Lebesch and Kimberly Jordan (who still recall the days of pulling up next to the sixteen-bay Budweiser delivery trucks to make deliveries in their Toyota), the brewery's production has grown from just over 800 barrels in 1992 to 30,000 in 1995. The family-run company claims that Fat Tire is the best-selling ale in Colorado. 500 Linden St., Fort Collins, CO (970) 221-0524.

Fat Tire Amber Ale

(og: 1.049; abw: 4.2%)

Malts/grains: Two-row Pale, Chocolate, Victory, Caramel 40L

With a short-lasting head, this smooth dry-hopped ale has a nutty malt flavor and mild hop bitterness. The name was inspired by a beer tasted on a mountain-biking trip.

Trippel Trappist Style Ale

(og: 1.073; abw: 6.8%)

Hops: Saaz

Malts/grains: Two-row Pale, Caramel 40L Victory

Brewed in the style of Belgian Trappist "triple" ale, this full-bodied golden ale is generously hopped with European Saaz.

Bottled beers not photographed:

Abbey Trappist Style Ale

(og: 1.064; abw: 5.5%)

Malts/grains: Two-row Pale, Chocolate, Victory, Caramel 80L, plus demerrera sugar

Old Cherry Ale

(og: 1.058; abw: 5%)

Malts/grains: Two-row Pale, Chocolate, Victory, Caramel 40L, plus Colorado Montmorency cherries

Sunshine Wheat Beer

(og: 1.048; abw: 4.2%)

Malts/grains: 50% Wheat, Two-row, plus coriander, orange peel

Oasis Brewery

The high style does not come at the expense of beers, which are very good indeed at Boulder's largest brewpub. Oasis opened downtown in 1992, and a brewery annex and tasting room were built on Walnut Street in late 1994 to handle increased production and distribution. Oasis Brewery and Restaurant, 1095 Canyon Blvd., Boulder, CO 80301, (303) 449-0363. Oasis Brewery Annex, 3201 Walnut St., #A, Boulder, CO 80301, (303) 440-8030.

Oasis Capstone Extra Special Bitter Ale

(og: 1.056; abw: 5%)

Hops: Nugget, Willamette

Malts/grains: Two-row Pale, British, Caramel, Roasted Barley

A powerful American interpretation of an English style bitter, this assertive, malty ale is packed with flavor.

Oasis Tut Brown Ale

(1.055; abw: 4.25%)

Hops: Cascade

Malts/grains: Two-row, Caramel, Black Patent

Somewhat light in flavor, this sweet, soft nut-brown ale has a roasted, malty flavor.

Oasis Zoser Oatmeal Stout

(og: 1.060; abw: 4.75%)

Hops: Centennial

Malts/grains: Two-row, Caramel, Black Patent, Chocolate, Roasted Barley, Oats

This robust, full-bodied stout is loaded with dark malts. Oatmeal is added for creaminess, and balanced by the tangy Centennial hops.

Bottled beers not photographed:

Oasis Pale Ale

(og: 1.051; abw: 4%)

Hops: Goldings

Malts/grains: Domestic Two-row, British, Caramel

Oasis Scarab Red

(og: 1.053; abw: 4%)

Hops: Mt. Hood

Malts/grains: Two-row Pale, British, Caramel, Roasted Pale

Rockies Brewing Company

Rockies Brewing Company (originally called Boulder Brewing Company) dates back to 1979 when it was founded in a goat shed on a farm near this college town. A post-modern facility was built in Boulder in 1984, and the name change in 1990 was accompanied by new ownership. Production between 1990 and 1994 increased more than 400% from 3,000 to 60,000 barrels per year. The ales are all-natural, brewed with Boulder Arapaho Glacier water. 2880 Wilderness Pl., Boulder, CO 80301, (303) 444-8448.

Boulder Amber Ale

(og: 1.054; abw: 3.6%)

Hops: Chinook, Cascade, Willamette

Malts/grains: Pale, Caramel 40L

The brewer's year-round favorite, this invigorating garnet-colored ale has a crisp hop finish.

Boulder Porter

(og: 1.056; abw: 3.6%)

Hops: Chinook, Hallertauer

Malts/grains: Pale, Crystal, Black Patent

Deep chocolate brown in color, this surprisingly light porter has dry coffee overtones and a soft, delicately-rounded body. Ideal for those who like a dark beer without the heavy bitter bite, it is good at mid-day or with winter meals.

Boulder Stout

(og: 1.066; abw: 4%)

Hops: Nugget, Willamette, Hallertauer

Malts/grains: Pale, Crystal, Chocolate, Black Patent

A dark, creamy, robust ale with a burnt chocolate finish and hearty flavor. A good winter repast.

Bottled beers not photographed:

Boulder Extra Pale Ale

(og: 1.054; abw: 3.8%)

Hops: Chinook, Cascade, Hallertauer

Malts/grains: Pale, Caramel 40L

Boulder Fall Fest Ale

seasonal

(og: 1.054)

Hops: Willamette, Mt. Hood

Malts/grains: Two-row Pale, Crystal 50L-60L, Black Patent, Roasted Barley

Buffalo Gold Premium Ale

(og: 1.051)

Hops: Nugget, Willamette, Cascade

Malts/grains: Two-row Pale, Crystal

Wrigley Red

(og: 1.056)

Hops: Nugget, Willamette, Cascade

Malts/grains: Pale, Crystal 20-80L, Roasted Barley

Telluride Beer Company

"People are upset when they hear that Telluride beer is contract brewed in Wisconsin," explained one distributor, "because they have a roman-tic view of Telluride and want the beer to come from there." (Tel-luride, in its mining heyday at the turn of the century, boasted five breweries, with one winning the Gold Medal at the 1902 World's Fair.) Started by Steve Patterson (who is now the brewmaster at Eddie McStiff's Brewpub in Moab, Utah), Telluride uses a recipe that hails from a beer brewed in Telluride until 1938. The beer is brewed at the Joseph Huber Brewery in Monroe, Wisconsin. Corporate office: P. O. Box 371623, Denver, CO 80231, (813) 961-7090.

Telluride Beer

(abw: 4.25)

A spritzy, light-tasting red that is hoppy and aromatic, with a generous mouth-feel and sharp finish.

Wynkoop Brewing Company

Wynkoop was started in 1988 by John Hick-enlooper, a geologist who had become intrigued with the West Coast brewpub scene during his travels while unemployed. The first brewpub to open in Colorado, Wynkoop still remains the largest beer-producing pub in the world (brewing 5,008 barrels in 1995). The pub also features a pool hall with regulation-size tables. 1634 18th Street, Denver, CO 80202, (303) 297-2700.

Railyard Ale

(og: 13.5, abw: 4.2%)

Hops: Hallertauer, Tettnanger

Malts: Pale, Crystal, Munich, Caramel

This amber-colored Oktoberfest is light and refreshing and the brewmaster's favorite of the 50 beers they brew. (This is the only one they bottle).

Great Northern Brewing Company

A fifth generation brewer, Minott Wessinger built his brewery in 1995 to brew a double-hopped lager (where hops are added at two stages of the brewing process). The beer is available in Montana and in the San Francisco Bay Area, where Wessinger lives. 2 Central Ave., Whitefish, MT 59937, (406) 863-1000.

Minott's Black Star Premium Lager Beer

(og: 1.049; abw: 3.9%)

Hops: Czech Saaz, Mt. Hood

Malts/grains: Two-row Pale, Caramel 60L, Malted Barley

A very good lager that opens aromatically and has a crisp refreshing flavor.

Bottled beers not photographed:

Wild Huckleberry Wheat Lager

(og: 1.007; abw: 5.8%)

Hops: Cascade

Malts/grains: Pale, Malted Wheat, plus huckleberry juice

Spanish Peaks Brewing Company

This brewery has been a popular spot since it opened in 1991 near the foot of the Spanish Peaks Mountain Range. The brewery has an attached ale house and Italian cafe where you can get homemade pizza and delicious beer fresh from the tap—bottled beers are contracted to August Schell Brewing Company in New Ulm, Minnesota. The black labrador retriever on the label is Chugwater Charlie Hill M.H., or "Chug" for short. 120 N. 19th St., Bozeman, MT 59715, (406) 585-2296.

Spanish Peaks Black Dog Ale

(og: 1.050, abw: 4.2%)

Malts/grains: Pale, Malted Barley, Munich, Crystal, Carastan, Chocolate

This English-style amber bitter is fresh tasting and lightly hopped—a good all-around porch drink.

Spanish Peaks Honey Raspberry Ale

(og: 1.046; abw: 3.92%)

A light bodied amber ale made with wildflower honey and natural raspberry—the raspberry taste and aroma are subtle, with the honey filling in the soft palate.

Bottled beers not photographed:

Sweetwater Wheat Ale

(og: 1.046; abw: 3.87%)

Hops: Noble

Malts/grains: Pale, Northwest Malted White Wheat

Yellowstone Pale Ale

(og: 1.056; abw: 4.78%)

Malts/grains: Pale, Crystal, Munich, Carastan

NEVADA

Holy Cow! Casino Cafe Brewery

Located on the Las Vegas strip (you can't miss the 14-by-20-foot Holstein above the entrance), this brewpub comes with slot machines and a frenetic energy that may make you think beer comes second, but don't be deceived. The brewery is managed by Tommy Almquist, a retired Air Force fighter pilot who makes an udderly great wheat beer. Producing 2,000 barrels per year, Holy Cow! also serves hefeweizen, stout, and seasonals in refillable growlers. 2423 Las Vegas Blvd., Las Vegas, NV 89102, (702) 732-2679.

Holy Cow! Amber Gambler Classic English Pale Ale

(og: 1.056; abw: 4.2%)

Hops: Fuggles, Cascade

Malts/grains: Two-row Caramel 40L, Munich, Carapils

Complex and floral, this English pale ale has a pronounced hoppiness and clean dry finish.

MT / NEVADA

Bottled beers not photographed:

Rebel Red English Brown

(og: 1.056; abw: 4.2%)

Hops: Fuggles

Malts/grains: Two-row Caramel 60L and 90L, Carapils

Holy Cow! Stout

(og: 1.062; abw: 5.5%)

Malts/grains: Two-row Caramel, Roasted Black Patent

Vegas Gold Hefe Weizen

(og: 1.050; abw: 4.2%)

Hops: Willamette

Malts/grains: Two-row Wheat, Carapils

OREGON

BridgePort Brewing Company

Established in 1984 as the Columbia River Brewing Company, the BridgePort Brewing Company is Oregon's oldest microbrewery. In 1986 a brewpub was built in the 19th-century warehouse that was once a hemp rope factory, featuring a menu of homemade pizzas (with crusts made from unfermented beer wort!) and seasonal beers on draft, including cask-conditioned ales (unfiltered ale that undergoes a second fermentation in the cask, a process that is rare among microbreweries and yields a richer flavor than regular ales). In 1984, the brewery produced 600 barrels per year; by 1994, it was producing 18,000 barrels per year; and now, it has the capacity to manufacture 60,000 barrels per year. The family-owned company was recently purchased by Gambrinus Incorporated. 1313 N.W. Marshall St., Portland, OR 97209, (503) 241-7179.

BridgePort Blue Heron Pale Ale

(og: 1.052; abw: 4.2%)

Hops: Willamette, Nugget

Malts/grains: Pale, Black Patent, Chocolate

Originally bottled as a fundraiser for the Portland Audubon Society, this label eventually inspired a "wetland" series of bird brews. There's nothing flighty about this medium bodied, amber-hued ale with its herbal tang and aroma. (Note: Outside of the Pacific Northwest, this ale is known as BridgePort Pale Ale.)

BridgePort Old Knucklehead Barley Wine Style Ale

seasonal

(og:1.096; abw: 8.7%)

Hops: Kent Goldings, Nuggets

Malts/grains: Pale, Scottish Crystal

Released every February, this hearty ale is aged like wine with double doses of malts and hops, producing a deep red color and sweet malty flavor. The label changes yearly to recognize people who exemplify the complexity of the brew; this particular label features former Portland mayor, J. E. "Bud" Clark.

BridgePort Pintail Extra Special Bitter Ale

(og: 1.056; abw: 5%)

Hops: Kent Goldings

Malts/grains: Scottish Pale

Copper-colored, this dry, aggressively hopped complex beer is edgier than some other ESBs, with a strong malt flavor, long finish, and aromatic nose.

OREGON

Bottled beers not photographed:

Coho Pacific Extra Pale Ale

(og: 1.044; abw: 3.6%)

Hops: Fuggles, Nugget

Malts/grains: Pale

Nut Brown Ale

(og: 1.048; abw: 4%)

Hops: Nugget, Northern Brewer, Willamette

Malts/grains: Pale

XX Stout Dublin Style

(og: 1.064; abw: 6%)

Hops: Northern Brewer, Fuggles

Malts/grains: Pale, Crystal, Black Patent

Deschutes Brewery

 At the Deschutes Brewery & Public House in Bend, you'll find cold-conditioned, unfiltered English-style ales on tap, as well as some lagers. (Cold-conditioning is a lagering process whereby the beer is set in a tank at a colder temperature, producing a clear, crisp beer.) The bottled beers are filtered to withstand the warm storage conditions, but they are bottled conditioned (where the yeast is left in the bottle and continues to ferment, causing a natural carbonation). Founded in 1988 (the first in Bend), the brewpub was so popular that brewery president Gary Fish began wholesale draft distribution in 1989, and the company has grown from 1,118 barrels in 1989 to 20,000 in 1994. The beer is distributed in Oregon, Washington, Idaho, Wyoming, Alaska, and Colorado, with more growth on the horizon; they recently completed a new brewing facility. The Brewery and Public House are located at 1044 N.W. Bond St., Bend, OR 97701, (541) 382-9242. The new brewing facility is located at 901 S.W. Simpson Ave., Bend, OR 97702, (541) 385-8606.

Bachelor Bitter

(og: 1.050; abw: 4%)

Hops: Galena, Willamette, Kent Goldings

Malts/grains: Pale, Crystal, Carapils

This dark red ale is slightly bitter, with a somewhat sweet, fruity character.

Black Butte Porter

(og: 1.056; abw: 4.5%)

Hops: Galena, Cascade, Tettnanger

Malts/grains: Pale, Chocolate, Crystal

This mild porter has a pleasing toastiness, with a lasting head and just enough hop bitterness to create an easy drinking beer.

Bottled beers not photographed:

Cascade Golden Ale

(og: 1.054; abw: 3.5%)

Hops: Galena, Tettnanger, Cascade

Malts/grains: Pale, Crystal, Carapils

Full Sail Brewing Company

Full Sail, which was the first Oregon microbrewery to offer bottled beer year-round, began brewing in 1987 and now has two locations: the Full Sail Brewing Company, which is located in a state-of-the-art plant built in 1995 in Hood River, and the Full Sail Brewery at the Riverplace Marina in Portland, a waterfront location next to McCormick & Schmick's Harborside Restaurant. Between the two plants, Full Sail produces about 31,000 barrels yearly. 506 Columbia St., Hood River, OR 97031, (541) 386-2281. 0307 S.W. Montgomery, Portland, OR 97201, (503) 222-5343.

Full Sail Amber Ale

(og: 1.059; abw: 4.7%)

Hops: Cascade, Mt. Hood

Malts/grains: Two-row Pale, Crystal, Chocolate

With an extravagant head and beautiful golden-brown color, this amber ale has a light mustiness and malt character, with a spicy floral hop finish. Delicious with pasta.

Full Sail Golden Ale

(og: 1.048; abw: 3.5%)

Hops: Mt. Hood, Tettnanger

Malts/grains: Two-row Pale, Crystal, Barley

With a golden caramel color and shallow head, this uncomplicated, mild beer begins with a slightly sweet taste, and ends with a zippy hop finish.

WasSail Winter Ale

winter seasonal

(og: 1.064; abw: 5.2%)

A heavy, molasses-colored ale in the traditional British "winter warmer" style, this slightly spicy ale is perfumed with aromas of toasted caramel, finishing with a bitter aftertaste. It's strong, and should be savored like brandy. Note the beautiful lacy head.

Bottled beers not photographed:

Full Sail Equinox ESB

spring seasonal

(abw: 4.5%)

Hops: English Target, Saaz

Malts/grains: Crystal

Full Sail India Pale

summer seasonal

(abw: 5%)

Hops: Challenger, Kent Goldings

Malts/grains: Two-row Triumph Pale

Full Sail Nut Brown Ale

(abw: 4.3%)

Hops: Domestic and imported

Malts/grains: Two-row Pale, Crystal, British Chocolate

Hair of the Dog Brewing Company

This Portland-based company is dedicated to unusual beer styles, and currently produces two: an Adambier (a revival of the old German Dortmund Adambier) and a Belgian tripel. Production is small (beers are numbered weekly), and the ales finish their conditioning in the bottle, which gives them a built-in shelf life; beers can be stored at room temperature and will continue to ferment slowly in the bottle, like wine, for several years. These ales are strong—beware the dog! 4509 S.E. 23rd Ave., Portland, OR 97202, (503) 232-6585.

Hair of the Dog Golden Rose Belgian Tripel Style Ale

(og: 1.074; abw: 6.5%)

Hops: Hallertauer

Malts/grains: Two-row Honey, Belgian Aromatic, plus candy sugar

A golden-colored, slightly fruity ale brewed with candy sugar.

Bottled beers not photographed:

Hair of the Dog Adambier

(og: 1.094; abw: 8%)

Hops: Northern Brewer, Tettnanger

Malts/grains: Gambrines, Two-row, Crystal, Black Patent, Chocolate, Peat, Munich

Nor'Wester Brewery & Public House

This growing Portland brewery began in 1993 with a goal of producing 10,000 barrels in 1994. They achieved that in the first three months, and by the end of 1994 had exceeded their capacity of 34,000 barrels per year. A new $3 million brewery is being built in Salem with a capacity of 80,000 barrels (expandable to 260,000 barrels), leaving the Portland brewery devoted to brewing draft exclusively for restaurants and bars. The company is publicly owned, with more than 8,000 shareholders who carry business cards identifying them as "founders," and information on the back of the card for restaurants who might want to order beer. The president is Jim Bernau, founder of one of Oregon's leading wineries as well as Microbreweries Across America, a development company that went public last year to build microbreweries in California, Washington, New York, and Georgia with Nor'Wester trained brewers, fermenters, yeast propagators, and other staff. 66 S.E. Morrison St., Portland, OR 97214, (800) 472-2739.

Nor'Wester Best Bitter Ale

(og: 1.054)

Hops: Oregon Willamette, Cascade, British Columbia Goldings

Malts/grains: Pale Barley, Imported Roasted Barley, Specialty

Modeled after English pub ales, this copper-colored ale is herbal and assertively hoppy, with characteristic bitterness.

Nor'Wester Hefe Weizen

(og: 1.048)

Hops: Oregon Mt. Hood, Tettnanger, German Hallertauer

Malts/grains: Pale Barley, Wheat, Specialty

This unfiltered wheat bear derives its straw-color and light palate from 55% wheat malt grist. A generous amount of fresh whole flower Oregon hops gives it a crisp spiciness.

Bottled beers not photographed:

Nor'Wester Blacksmith Porter

(og: 1.051)

Hops: Oregon Willamette

Malts/grains: Pale Barley, Roasted Barley

Nor'Wester Dunkel Weizen

(og: 1.050)

Hops: Mt. Hood, Tettnanger, German Hallertauer

Malts/grains: Wheat, Barley, Roasted Barley

Nor'Wester Peach Creme Ale

(og: 1.048)

Hops: Mt. Hood

Malts/grains: Two-row Barley, Malted Wheat, Light Roasted Barley, plus red peach concentrate

Nor'Wester Raspberry Weizen

og:1.048)

Hops: Mt. Hood

Malts/grains: Two-row Barley, Malted Wheat, Light Roasted Barley

Nor'Wester Winter Weizen

winter seasonal

(og: 1.064)

Hops: Kent Goldings, Willamette

Malts/grains: Scottish Floor Malted Barley, Light Roasted Barley, Torrified Wheat

Oregon Ale and Beer Company

While working for the Boston Beer Company in Oregon, Gregg LeBlanc and Duke Maines fell in love with the beer scene. "The people here are the most knowledgeable and adventurous beer drinkers in America," claims Maines. With funding from Boston Beer Company investors, they formed the Oregon Ale and Beer Company in 1994 with a goal of brewing classic ales with local hops, and production quickly leapt to 30,000 barrels per year. They date-stamp all beers, which are brewed at several local facilities (including the Saxer brewery, located across the street from their corporate office). Passionate about beer, LeBlanc concedes he's come a long way since his brother handed him a "Spoodie Odie" (a mixture of Boone's Farm Apple Wine and Schlitz) at the age of thirteen. Corporate office: 5755 Southwest Jean Rd., Lake Oswego, OR 97035, (503) 968-7706.

Oregon Hefeweizen

(og: 1.048; abw: 4.2%)

Hops: Northern Brewer, Willamette

Malts/grains: Two-row Caramel 60L, Wheat

Brewed with wheat malt, this crisp, light, unfiltered wheat ale has a subtle fruitiness. Good at barbecues or with fresh fish.

Bottled beers not photographed:

Honey Red Ale

(og: 1.053; abw: 4.3%)

Hops: Mt. Hood, Ultra

Malts/grains: Two-row Caramel 60L, Munich

Nut Brown Ale

(og: 1.050; abw: 4.2%)

Hops: Northern Brewer, Willamette

Malts/grains: Two-row Caramel 60L, Special Roast, Roasted Barley, Victory

Oregon Original India Pale Ale

(og: 1.055; abw: 4.4%)

Hops: Northern Brewer, Cascade, Saaz

Malts/grains: Two-row Caramel 60L, Wheat

Raspberry Wheat

(og: 1.051; abw: 4.1%)

Hops: Northern Brewer, Willamette

Malts/grains: Two-row Caramel 60L, Wheat

Oregon Brewing Company

With some of the coolest labels in the business, the Oregon Brewing Company continues to assert itself as a great beer maker and savvy marketer. Established in 1989, Rogue Ales and specialty beers are now available in 30 states, and devotees are evangelical about the beer. The brewmaster is John Maier, 1988 Homebrewer of the Year and self-described bon vivant, who leads a "dedicated crew of spiritualists." The winner of a handful of GABF medals (their Rogue smoke is to die for), Rogue produces 20,000 barrels per year, and has four facilities in two locations: in Newport you'll find the brewery, the Rogue Gallery & Public House, and the House of Rogues Tasting Room. In Ashland, Rogue operates a brewpub near the Shakespeare Theater. Rogue Brewery, 2320 OSU Dr., Newport, OR 97365, (541) 867-3660. Rogue Gallery and Public House, 746 S.W. Bay Blvd., Newport, OR 97365, (541) 265-3118. House of Rogues Tasting Room, 3135 S.E. Ferry Slip Rd., Newport, OR 97365, (541) 867-4131. Rogue Brewery & Public House, 31-B Water St., Ashland, OR 97520, (541) 488-5061.

Rogue Dead Guy Ale

fall seasonal

Hops: Perle, Saaz

Malts/grains: Harrington, Klages, Carastan, Munich

In the maibock style with an ale yeast, Dead Guy is mahogany-colored and released at Halloween—hence the bats and spider webs on the label. With a wonderful lacy head, this ale has a sweet aroma that makes its way slowly to your nose, and a long finish. (Dead Guy is identical to Rogue MaierBock.)

Rogue Shakespeare Stout

Hops: Cascade

Malts/grains: Northwest Klages, Harrington, Crystal, Beeston, Chocolate, Roasted Barley, Rolled Oats

Originally brewed at the Ashland brewpub in honor the Shakespeare Theater, this chewy ebony-colored stout has a foamy head that builds and lingers. The taste is robust and redolent of coffee, with a mellow chocolate aftertaste and a long bitter finish. Rogue has released a limited edition of this stout for St. Patrick's Day and renamed it Wild Irish Rogue—it features a picture of Dick Lytle of Mt. Hood Beverage and is "dedicated to the Dick in each of us." (I bet the p.r. person had to do some backpedaling on that one.)

St. Rogue Red Ale

(og: 1.052; abw: 4.2%)

Hops: Chinook, Centennial

Malts/grains: Two-row Harrington, Klages, Hugh Baird, Carastan, Crystal, Munich

Brewed in honor of Gambrinus, this is a serious beer, with a marvelous yeasty bouquet, a roasty malt flavor, and hoppy spruce finish. A hop head's delight, this wondrously fresh brew has a beautiful copper color with a foamy off-white head. Enjoy with turkey sandwiches on dark bread.

Bottled beers not photographed:

American Amber

(og: 1.052; abw: 4.2%)

Hops: Oregon Cascade

Malts/grains: Two-row Crystal, Caramel

Hefeweizen

summer seasonal

Hops: Saaz

Malts/grains: Barley, Wheat, plus coriander, ginger

Mexicali Rogue

(og: 1.052, abw: 4.2%)

Hops: Willamette, Cascade

Malts/grains: Harrington, Klages, Munich, plus chipotle chiles

Mogul Ale

pale ale

(og: 1.066; abw: 5.2%)

Hops: Perle, Saaz, Centennial, Cascade, Willamette, Chinook

Malts/grains: Northwest Harrington, Munich, Crystal, Chocolate

Old Crustacean

barleywine

(og: 10.104; abw: 9%)

Hops: Chinook, Centennial

Malts/grains: Northwest Harrington, Crystal, Munich

Oregon Golden Ale

(og: 1.052; 4.2%)

Hops: Willamette

Malts/grains: Northwest Harrington, Munich

Rogue Mocha Porter

(og: 1.052; abw: 4.2%)

Hops: Perle, Centennial

Malts/grains: Northwest Harrington, Chocolate, Crystal, Munich

Rogue-N-Berry

(og: 1.048; abw: 3.8%)

Hops: Saaz

Malts/grains: Northwest Harrington, Carastan, Chocolate, plus marion berries

Rogue Smoke

(og: 1.058; abw: 5%)

Hops: Perle, Saaz

Malts/grains: Northwest Harrington, Crystal, Carastan, Hand-smoked Munich

St. Rogue Dry Hopped

(og: 1.052; abw: 4.2%)

Hops: Raw Centennial

Malts/grains: Two-row Harrington, Klages, Hugh Baird, Carastan, Crystal, Munich

Youngers Special Bitter

(og: 1.048; abw: 3.8%)

Hops: Willamette, Kent Goldings

Malts/grains: Two-row Harrington, Crystal

Oregon Trail Brewery

When I called this tiny (1,200 barrel per year) brewery, the answering machine referred me to Fresh Hops, a homebrew shop 12 miles down the road, where Dave Wills serves as president of both ventures. Just off Interstate 5, the brewery shares space with a deli ("We're sort of a fake brewpub," explains Wills, "which allows us to focus on making beer, not chili.") Started by homebrewers in 1987, Oregon Trail beer is presently available only in Oregon, but Wills is negotiating with a contract brewer so that he might expand into other western states. 341 S.W. Second St., Corvallis, OR 97339-0070, (503) 758-3527.

Oregon Trail White Ale

(og: 1.043; abw: 3.5%)

Hops: Perle, Mt. Hood

Malts/grains: Pale, Wheat, Crystal

In addition to Barley malt, wheat, and hops, this wheat beer is spiced with coriander and dried orange peel. (The white haze is brewer's yeast, and it's fine to drink.)

Saxer Brewing Company

Henry Saxer was one of the first brewers in the Northwest, opening his Portland brewery in 1852. The new Saxer Brewing Company was established in 1992 to carry on his name and tradition of brewing German-style lagers, and is currently Oregon's only microbrewery dedicated exclusively to doing so. Brewmaster Tony Gomes lagers the beers at cold temperatures for at least 30 days. 5875 S.W. Lakeview Blvd., Lake Oswego, OR 97035, (503) 699-9524.

Saxer Lemon Lager

(og: 1.040; abw: 2.8%)

Hops: Yakima Valley Perle, Czech Saaz

Malts/grains: Two-row Pale

Lagered with lemon juice extract, this quaffable beer is the color of ginger ale, with a quick-dissolving head. Good for country picnics or easy drinking on a summer day.

Saxer Three Finger Jack Hefedunkel

(og: 1.050; abw: 4.10%)

Hops: German Hersbrucker

Malts/grains: Two-row Munich, Caramel, Black Patent

With a creamy head, this garnet-colored lager is slightly malty, with a light hop taste passing over the taste buds.

Bottled beers not photographed:

Saxer Three Finger Jack-Amber

(abw: 4%)

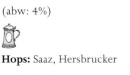

Hops: Saaz, Hersbrucker

Malts/grains: Seven-row Pale, Munich, Dark Carapils

Saxer Three Finger Jack-Stout

(abw: 4.8%)

Malts/grains: Two-row Pale, Munich, Roasted Barley

Star Brewing Company

Opened in 1983 on the north side of town by Scott Wenzel, this tiny (3,500 barrel) brewery sells 75% of its beer out of state, interestingly enough. "The Big Five take care of most of the beer in the state," says sales manager Jeff Markee, referring to Deschutes, Full Sail, and other older breweries, "and we find that outside the state people are craving Oregon products." 5231 N.E. Martin Luther King Blvd., Portland, OR 97211, (503) 282-6003.

Star Brewing Black Cherry Stout

(og: 1.060; abw: 5%)

Hops: Northern Brewer, Tettnanger

Malts/grains: Munich, Wheat, Crystal 80L, Two-row Roasted Barley, plus black cherries

Fresh Oregon black cherries provide a wonderful backdrop for the lively malt and chocolate flavors.

Star Brewing Raspberry Wheat Ale

(og: 1.050; abw: 3.92%)

Hops: Wheat, Liberty

Malts/grains: Munich, Two-row Carastan 30-37L

This ale fermented with Oregon raspberries has a dry champagne finish and plenty of raspberry flavor and aroma. It's a summery drink.

Bottled beers not photographed:

Bright Star Pineapple Ale

(og: 1.048; abw: 4.15%)

Hops: Mt. Hood, Liberty

Malts/grains: Munich, Two-row Carastan 30-37L

Dark Star Nut Brown Ale

(og: 1.052; abw: 3.98%)

Hops: Northern Brewer, Tettnanger, Perle

Malts/grains: Pale, Munich, Crystal 50-60L, Chocolate, Wheat

Widmer Brothers Brewing Company

The first microbrewery in the Northwest to focus on German-style ales (which even in Germany are relatively rare), family-owned Widmer was started by two brothers in 1984 with a special Bavarian yeast and a penchant for German brewing techniques. One of their first beers was hefeweizen, a golden, cloudy unfiltered beer kegged directly from the lagering tank which, according to the Oregon Liquor Control Commission, was Oregon's top-selling draft microbrew in 1995. Popular at ski resorts, Widmer in 1996 relinquished its status as the country's largest draft-only brewery (producing 130,000 barrels per year) when it started bottling beer. The company's on-site Gasthaus offers a full view of the brew house and fermentation room. Widmer contracts with a plant in Milwaukee to brew for its Eastern markets. 929 North Russell, Portland, OR 97227, (503) 281-BIER.

Widmer Blackbier

(abw: 5%)

Hops: Perle, Tettnanger

Malts/grains: Caramel, Chocolate, Black Patent, Roasted Barley

Full-bodied, with the richness of a stout but the drinkability of a porter, this was originally a winter seasonal but its popularity led Widmer to brew it year round. A warming black beer for cool nights, it holds up well with beef tenderloin and rib eye steak.

Widmer Hefeweizen

(og: 1.047; abw: 3.4%)

Hops: Tettnanger, Cascade

Malts/grains: Caramel, Munich

The Bavarian yeast and Northwest hops are evident in this golden, unfiltered beer with a clean taste. Serve it with spicy foods.

UTAH

Schirf Brewing Company

The beer of choice at the Sundance Film Festival, Schirf was established in 1986 in Salt Lake City. A new facility has enabled Schirf to triple production (with current capacity of 100,000 barrels per year). The company also operates the Wasatch Brew Pub in Park City, which produces 4,900 barrels per year for on-site consumption. Brewmaster Mike Mankoschwski trained at the Paulaner-Thomass Brewery in Munich. Their flagship Wasatch Premium Ale is succeeding despite the Mormons (when president Greg Schirf met with the Utah Alcoholic Beverage and Control Division in the mid 1980s, they told him they weren't sure if breweries were legal). "Half the people in Utah don't drink beer," says Schirf, "so it's incumbent on the rest of us to make up for that." 1763 South 300 West, Salt Lake City, UT 84115, (801) 645-9500. (Wasatch Brew Pub is located at 250 Main St., Park City, UT 84060, (801) 645-9500.)

Wasatch Premium Ale

(og: 1.040; abw: 4%)

Hops: Chinook, Cascade

Malts/grains: Two-row Crystal, Vienna, Chocolate, Wheat Malt, Carapils

Golden brown, with a low head, this is an aromatic pale ale, with a flowery aroma and good fruitiness.

Wasatch Raspberry Wheat Beer

(og: 1.040; abw: 4%)

Hops: Chinook, Willamette, Tettnanger, Perle

Malts/grains: Wheat, Two-row Crystal, Carapils

With a long-lasting lazy head, this cloudy fruity beer is the color of canola oil, with a beautiful raspberry nose, a short-lived berry taste, and a fruity bitter finish.

Wasatch Slickrock Lager

(og: 1.040; abw: 4%)

Hops: Czech Saaz, Cascade

Malts/grains: Two-row Vienna, Carapils, Wheat Malt

The head was in a hurry in this light, crisp hoppy lager that glistens like 14-karat gold. Local mountain bikers discovered its thirst-quenching appeal and nicknamed it "biker beer."

Bottled beers not photographed:

Wasatch Irish Stout

(og: 1.040; abw: 4%)

Hops: Chinook, Cascade

Malts/grains: Two-row Wheat Malt, Crystal, Chocolate, Black Patent, Munich

Wasatch Weizenbier

(og: 1.040; abw: 4%)

Hops: Chinook, Willamette, Tettnanger, Perle

Malts/grains: Two-row Wheat Malt, Crystal, Carapils

WASHINGTON

Big Time Brewing Company

Located in the University district of Seattle since 1988, this brewpub is owned by Reid Martin, who also maintains the popular Triple Rock brewpub in Berkeley, California. Located in a 19th-century building, the pub features much breweriana on the walls and, like its Berkeley sister, gets raves on the Internet for brewing beers that are loaded with flavor. 4133 University Way N.E., Seattle, WA 98105, (206) 545-4509.

WASHINGTON

Bhagwan's Best India Pale Ale

(og: 1.064; abw: 5%)

Over the top with hop flavor and a complex, long-lasting floral nose, this malty American-style IPA is a real pleasure. Dry-hopped and cask-conditioned, with a thick rich head and toasted orange color, this unfiltered ale is a particular treat pulled from the hand pump at Big Time.

Coal Creek Porter

(og: 1.060; abw: 4.5%)

Hops: Yakima, Centennial

Impenetrably dark chocolate at first glance, Coal Creek reveals red highlights under the light. With a creamy rich head, the taste has a big build up, with malty character and a hoppy finish. A blend of dark roasted and specialty malts give it a roasted flavor and smooth texture.

Old Wooly Barleywine Ale

winter seasonal

(abw: 9.5%)

Anticipated throughout the fall in the Seattle area and released on December 1, Old Wooly is Big Time's biggest and rarest beer. The recipe varies yearly, although—true to a barleywine—it's always powerfully malty, balanced by a prodigious amount of hops.

Bottled beers not photographed:

Atlas Amber Ale

(og: 1.056; abw: 4%)

Hops: Chinook, Cascade, Centennial

Malts/grains: Pale, Crystal, Munich, plus light dextrin

Prime Time Pale Ale

(og: 1.048; abw: 3%)

Hops: Yakima Chinook, Cascade, Hersbrucker

Malts/grains: Northwestern Two-role Pale, English Crystal, plus light dextrin

Fort Spokane Brewery

Located near the confluence of the Spokane and Columbia rivers, the Fort Spokane Brewery is named after the Fort Spokane Brewery of 1889, which produces beer in the German alt style. (Altbier means "old beer" in German, referring to the way beer was made before the discovery of lager yeast—namely, by fermenting beer with ale yeast then condition-ing it at cold temperatures.) Back in the 1880s, Ben Bockemuehl made altbier from local barley and hops, cold-conditioning it in an ice cave before delivering it to the troops. Today, the Fort Spokane Brewery (established by Bockemuehl's grandson in 1989) makes altbier by lagering it at 45° for over a week, creating a complex mellow flavor. 401 West Spokane Falls Blvd., Spokane, WA 99201, (509) 838-3809.

Fort Spokane Border Run

(og: 1.056; abw: 5.6%)

Hops: Willamette, Yakima, Tettnanger

Malts/grains: Two-row Pale, Munich, Washington White Wheat

With a thin head, this mahogany-colored ale has a bouquet that fills your nose and mouth, and a wonderful peachy-oak finish. The brewer proclaims it "like a slice of liquid bread from Dusseldorf." Amen.

WASHINGTON

Bottled beers not photographed:

Blonde Alt

(og: 1.052; abw: 5.6%)

Hops: Willamette, Tettnanger

Malts/grains: Pale, Munich, Wheat, Caramel

Bulldog Stout

(og: 1.056; abw: 5%)

Hops: Willamette

Malts/grains: Pale, Roasted Barley, Flaked Barley, Caramel, Black Patent

Red Alt

(og: 1.052; abw: 5%)

Hops: Willamette

Malts/grains: Pale, Caramel, Munich, Chocolate

Hart Brewing Company

One of the granddaddies of the microbrewery movement, the Hart Brewing Company was founded in 1984 when a married couple opened a brewery in a 19th-century general store in Kalama, a small logging town squeezed between the Columbia River and the foothills of Mt. St. Helens. Known for its excellent fly fishing and the glacial waters (which became a key ingredient in the beers), Kalama is just over the mountains from the Yakima Valley, one of the world's greatest hop-growing regions. Production of Pyramid Pale Ale (named after the ancient Egyptians who were among the first to brew beer) started at 200 barrels the first year. The company, which specialized in British ales and German wheat beers, saw steady growth and new ownership through the late 1980s and, in 1992, acquired the Thomas Kemper Brewery, dedicated to producing authentic German lagers. By 1995, Hart Brewing was brewing over 100,000 barrels per year, with demand prompting brewing facilities in three locations: Poulsboro, Kalama, and Seattle. The company continues to turn out unpasteurized beer made only with the classic ingredients as well as fruit beers made with natural extracts and purées. Pyramid Ales Brewery, 110 West Marine Dr., Kalama, WA 98625, (206) 673-2121. Hart Brewery and Pub, 1201 1st Ave. S., Seattle, WA 98134, (206) 682-3377.

Hart Espresso Stout

(og: 1.062; abw: 4.5%)

Hops: Nugget, Liberty

Malts/grains: Two-row Caramel, Munich, Roasted Barley, Black Patent

With a rocky, tawny-colored head and layers of coffee and chocolate flavors, this jet-black bitter ale is ashy, dense, and well-named. Suitable for hearty Italian food, steak, and chocolate, or sipping by the fire. (It's brewed with dark malts, not espresso beans.)

Pyramid Apricot Ale

(og: 1.045; abw: 3.95%)

Hops: Nugget, Perle

Malts/grains: Two-row Caramel, Wheat

This ale combines hefeweizen with the natural essence of apricots to create a tangy, hazy wheat beer with a powerful apricot aroma and more subtle apricot flavor. Delicious with grilled fish or with spicy curries.

WASHINGTON

Pyramid Hefeweizen Ale

(og: 1.045; abw: 3.95%)

Hops: Nugget, Perle

Malts/grains: Two-row Wheat, Caramel

Having disappeared during prohibition, wheat beers were resurrected in the 1980s by Hart Brewing. Made with locally-grown wheat and hops, this straw-colored, slightly cloudy beer is delicate and light, with a pleasant citric fizziness and refreshing finish.

Pyramid Pale Ale

(og: 1.048; abw: 3.95%)

Hops: Cascade

Malts/grains: Two-row Caramel

Known as Special Bitter on draft in the Northwest, this nutty dark-copper colored ale is rich, tangy, and full of flavor, with a satisfying finish. Sure to hold its own with spicy dishes or at barbecues.

Bottled beers not photographed:

Pyramid Best Brown Ale

(og: 1.052; abw: 3.95%)

Hops: Nugget, Liberty

Malts/grains: Two-row Caramel, Munich, Dark Carastan, Roasted Barley

Pyramid Wheaten Ale

(og: 1.042; abw: 3.95%)

Hops: Nugget, Perle

Malts/grains: Two-row Caramel, Wheat

Pike Pub and Brewing Company

This cool microbrewery in Seattle's historic Pike Place district is owned by Tom Leavitt and beer guru Charles Finkel, a graphic designer who not only founded Merchant du Vin (a highly esteemed importer of great ales from England and Belgium, and bocks and pilsners from Germany) but has an irresistible museum of breweriana next door to the pub. Established in 1989, Pike Brewing was one of the first U.S. breweries to cask-condition its ales, and still does its own malting. Finkel brews about 25,000 barrels per year and experiments with many styles—including a Five Grain Speltsbier that he brewed from a 17th-century recipe for the opening of an Old Dutch Masters Exhibit at the Seattle Art Museum. Beer connoisseur Michael Jackson listed Pike among eight breweries whose beers he would want if stranded on a desert island. 1415 First Ave., Seattle, WA 98101, (206) 622-6044.

Pike Auld Acquaintance Spiced Ale

winter seasonal

(og: 1.052; abw: 3.6%)

Hops: Clusters, Goldings

Malts/grains: Two-row Pale, Crystal

Brewed for the holidays, this ale is subtly spiced with cinnamon, nutmeg, zested fresh orange peel, and coriander seed. A mellow, well-rounded amber ale that is perfect for winter nights or a festive meal.

Pike Pale Ale

(og: 1.052; abw: 3.8%)

Hops: Goldings

Malts/grains: Two-row Pale, Crystal

Unfiltered and unpasteurized, this full bodied classic pale ale has a nutty malt flavor and assertive hop character. With a deep copper color, it is rounded and mellow, with the delicate fruity esters of peach and apricot. Brewed using the traditional English single-infusion mash and copper $4^1/_2$ barrel brewkettle, this pale ale is good with seafood, mussel stew, fried oysters, or aged cheddar and apples.

WASHINGTON

Pike Street Stout

(og: 1.072; abw: 4.8%)

Hops: Chinook, Goldings

Malts/grains: Crisp Maris Otter, Two-row Pale, Crystal, Roasted Barley

A stout lover's stout, this ale is painstakingly brewed to the traditional Dublin style (aged over six weeks before release). With a deep chocolate color and smooth malt texture, this full-bodied beer has a strong hoppiness that gives it a clean finish.

Bottled beers not photographed:

Pike IPA

(og: 1.064; abw: 5.2%)

Hops: Chinook, Goldings

Malts/grains: Two-row Pale, Crystal, Munich, Carapils

Pike Old Bawdy Barley Wine

winter seasonal

(og: 1.096; abw: 7.9%)

Malts/grains: Two-row Pale, Peated, Crystal, Roasted Barley

Pike Porter

winter seasonal

(og: 1.045; abw: 3.2%)

Hops: Clusters, Goldings

Malts/grains: Two-row Pale, Crystal, Carapils, Munich, Biscuit, Special-B, Chocolate, Black Patent

Redhook Ale Brewery

In 1980, Starbucks founder Gordon Bowker was working on a wine project with Paul Shipman when both became intrigued with the idea of brewing a local beer. They were impressed by the early ventures of New Albion, and thought there might be a market for craft brewing in Seattle (their market research also revealed that Washington State beer drinkers consume more draft beer per capita than any other state). Forming the Independent Ale Brewery in 1981 (later known as Redhook Ale Brewery) in Seattle's Scandinavian neighborhood, they started making British ales in 1982. Bottled beers were introduced in 1985 and Redhook's phenomenal success (a 40% annual growth rate during its first nine years) encouraged the company to build two new brewing facilities. In 1994, Anheuser-Busch bought 20% of the company. (By the way, the name Redhook came from the color of the original ale and a desire to "hook" the consumer.) 3400 Phinney Ave., Seattle, WA 98103, (206) 548-8000.

Red Hook ESB Extra Special Bitter Ale

(og: 1.054; abw: 4.3%)

Hops: Willamette, Tettnanger

Malts/grains: Two-row Klages, Caramel 60L

Redhook's most popular beer, this well-balanced bitter is tangy and flavorful, with a soft mouth-feel, ringing hoppiness, and sweet finish. A beautiful transparent deep-amber colored brew, it's good with fowl, game, or imported cheeses.

Red Hook Rye

(og: 1.052; abw: 4%)

Hops: Mt. Hood, Yakima Hersbrucker

Malts/grains: Two-row Klages, Munich Malt, Flaked Rye

Brewed with flaked rye, this unfiltered ale is best enjoyed by "relaxing the yeast" which means laying the bottle on its side and gently rolling it to release the grain flavor back into the ale. (For a subtler quaff, decant it.) The spicy character is complemented by the full grain flavors.

Bottled beers not photographed:

Blackhook Porter

(og: 1.049; abw: 3.9%)

Hops: Willamette, Eroica, Cascade

Malts/grains: Two-row Klages, Caramel 40L, Black Patent, Roasted Barley

Double Black Stout

(og: 1.073; abw: 6.2%)

Hops: Chinook, Northern Brewer

Malts/grains: Two-row Klages, Munich, Black Patent, Malted Wheat, Roasted Barley, plus Starbucks coffee

Wheat Hook Ale

(og: 1.046; abw: 3.8%)

Hops: Mt. Hood, Willamette, Yakima Hersbrucker

Malts/grains: Two-row Klages, Malted Wheat, Munich Malt

Ya Sure Ya Betcha Ballard Bitter

(og: 1.059; abw: 4.7%)

Hops: Northern Brewer, Willamette, Cascade

Malts/grains: Two-row Klages, Caramel 40L, Munich

Thomas Kemper Brewery

Located in a beautiful valley near the Scandinavian-settled town of Poulsbo (just a short ferry ride across Puget Sound from Seattle), the Thomas Kemper Brewery was founded with the goal of producing distinctive German-style lagers. Kemper more recently expanded to include several Bavarian-inspired weizenbiers and seasonal beers, which are brewed next to the Tap Room and Beer Garden where English and German pub fare is served. Founded in 1985, the company was bought by Hart Brewing in 1992. Bottled Thomas Kemper lagers are produced in Poulsbo as well as the Hart Brewery in Seattle. 22381 Foss Rd., Poulsbo, WA 98370, (360) 697-1446.

Thomas Kemper Dark Lager

(og: 1.058; abw: 4.5%)

Hops: Nugget, Styrian

Malts/grains: Two-row Munich, Chocolate, Caramel 40 and 80L

First brewed in Munich in the 1830s, early lagers were dark brown and became known as the "Munchener" style. Thomas Kemper is helping to revive the tradition of good old-fashioned lagers with this unusual beer that will do much to win back the lager's good name. Dark like a port, with a beautiful fresh bouquet suggestive of tangerines, this reddish-brown lager is full-tasting, with a malty-sweet flavor balanced by the spicy Styrian finishing hops. Good with steaks, chops, and hearty foods.

Thomas Kemper Hefeweizen

(og: 1.050; abw: 4%)

Hops: Nugget, Liberty

Malts/grains: Two-row Wheat

This cloudy unfiltered wheat beer is fresh and light, with a soft yeasty aroma and aromatic effervescence from the unfiltered yeast. Appealing with seafood and salads.

Thomas Kemper Weizenberry

(og: 1.050; abw: 4%)

Hops: Nugget, Liberty

Malts/grains: Two-row Wheat

Once called "the champagne of the North," German wheat beers date back to the 19th-century. Crisp and effervescent, they are the perfect summer brew, and often sweetened in Europe with a dash of fruit syrup. Here Thomas Kemper adds the fruit in the brewing process, creating a pale golden lager with a huge raspberry bouquet and very subtle (almost indistinguishable) raspberry flavor. Serve with dessert or ice cream.

Bottled beers not photographed:

Thomas Kemper Amber Lager

(og: 1.052; abw: 4%)

Hops: Nugget, Liberty, Saaz

Malts/grains: Two-row Munich, Caramel 40L and 80L

Thomas Kemper Honey Weizen

(og: 1.050; abw: 4%)

Hops: Nugget, Liberty

Malts/grains: Pale, Wheat

Thomas Kemper Pale Lager

(og: 1.048; abw: 3.5%)

Hops: Nugget, Liberty

Malts/grains: Two-row Munich, Black Patent, Caramel 40L

Yakima Brewing

In one of the world's largest hop-growing regions, Yakima Brewing was founded in 1982 by Bert Grant, a Scotsman who has been in the beer business for more than 50 years. He opened Grant's Brewery Pub (one of the nation's first brewpubs) as well, whose popularity led Bert to expand to a new brewery and relocate the pub to a 19th-century train station (which serves, among other things, fish and chips and British bangers). According to The Erickson Report, Yakima Brewing has been sold to a large holding company representing the Chateau St. Michelle Winery, and founder Bert Grant remains as brewmaster. All his beers are highly hopped. 1803 Presson Pl., Yakima, WA 98902, (509) 575-1900. (Grant's Brewery Pub is located at 32 N. Front St., Yakima, WA 98901, (509) 575-2922.)

Grant's Imperial Stout

(og: 1.070; abw: 6.2%)

Hops: Galena, Cascade

Malts/grains: Pale, Black Patent, Caramel, plus honey

Dark as a moonless night, this husky stout is heavy and complex, with notes of chocolate and coffee, and a malty bittersweetness from the Barley. With a frothy cappuccino-like head and pleasant density, it will stand up to espresso or sharp cheeses.

Grant's Scottish Ale

(og: 1.01; abw: 4.7%)

Hops: Cascade

Malts/grains: Pale, Caramel

A heavy, aggressively-hopped ale with medium maltiness and a hint of cloves. Good with smoked meats or hearty sandwiches.

Grant's Weis Beer

(og: 1.046; abw: 4.2%)

Hops: Cascade

Malts/grains: Pale, Wheat

Mildly fruity in the weizen beer tradition, this nimble beer has a mild bitterness that holds its own with strong flavors.

Bottled beers not photographed:

Grant's Apple Honey Ale

(og: 1.044; abw: 3%)

Hops: Cascade

Malts/grains: Pale, plus honey and apple concentrate

Grant's Celtic Ale

(og: 1.034; abw: 2.4%)

Hops: Cascade

Malts/grains: Pale, Caramel, Black Patent

Grant's India Pale Ale

(og: 1.046; abw: 3.3%)

Hops: Galena, Cascade

Malts/grains: Pale

Grant's Perfect Porter

(og: 1.048; abw: 3.1%)

Hops: Willamette

Malts/grains: Pale, Chocolate, Caramel, Peat, Black Patent

WYOMING

Otto Brothers' Brewing Company

Geologists by training, homebrewers Charlie and Ernie Otto went into business in 1988. Of Austrian-German descent, they loved European beers, and vowed to make beer with no chemical preservatives or pasteurization processes. Recalling Wyoming's rich brewing tradition dating back to 1868 when two gold rush breweries quenched the thirst of South Pass City miners, they feature "growlers," which originally referred to tin pails that customers at tap stations would fill up, clean out, and re-use. The concept has flourished again in Western states since the Ottos rekindled the idea with a 64-ounce glass jug version. The first microbrewery in Wyoming since 1954, Otto Brothers' is located just west of Jackson in a Swiss chalet-style building designed by the brothers. 1295 Northwest St., Wilson, WY 83014, (307) 733-9000.

Otto Brothers' Moose Juice Stout

(abw: 5.9%)

Hops: Chinook, Cascade

Malts/grains: Munich, Chocolate, Caramel, Roasted Barley

Dark and cloudy with a medium-lasting but full head, this dry stout has a strong malt flavor with a slight bitterness and hint of chocolate.

Otto Brothers' Teton Ale

(og: 1.048; abw: 4.5%)

Malts/grains: Caramel, Munich, Roasted Barley

Otto's flagship, this English-style amber ale has a rich copper color and a lasting head, with a sharp hoppy finish.

Bottled beers not photographed:

Otto Brothers' Old Faithful Ale

Hops: Cascade, Willamette

Malts/grains: Barley

Snake River Brewing Company

When the first mountain men arrived in Jackson in the mid-1800s, they declared the "hole" uninhabitable due to the severe winters. Little did they know that within the next century Jackson Hole would be a winter playland where everyone skis—including the head brewer at Snake River Brewing. The company was started by Albert Upsher, a former securities analyst from Manhattan. He owned an Anheuser-Busch distributorship for 11 years before opening Snake River with his wife Joni in 1994. The brewery is located in their Jackson Hope Pub & Brewery, which claims the title of Wyoming's first brewpub (for beer aficionados, the first brewery title since 1954 goes to neighboring Otto Brothers). Snake River's beer is brewed in 30-barrel quantities to maintain quality control. An expansion in 1996 allowed them to increase output to 10,000 barrels per year. 265 S. Millward, Jackson, WY 83001-7000, (307) 739-2337.

Snake River Pale Ale

(og: 1.050; abw: 5.4%)

Hops: Washington Chinook, Washington Cascade

Malts/grains: Munich 7L, Pale, Carastan 34L

With a creamy head and butterscotch color, this delicious classic pale ale has a hoppy nose and slightly malty start with a bitter hops finish.

Snake River Zonker Stout

(og: 1.060; abw: 5.7%)

Hops: Chinook, Kent Goldings, Washington Willamette

Malts/grains: Chocolate, Black Patent, Carastan 34L, Pale, Caramel 75L, Malt 150L

This velvety stout has a generous amount of roasted Barley, with the hops lending a mild bitterness.

Bottled beers not photographed:

Snake River Lager

(abw: 5.6%)

Hops: Washington, Perle, Tettnanger

Malts/grains: Two-row Pale, Munich 7L, Carastan 34L, Caramel 75L and 150L

MIDWEST

The heart of American brewing in the 19th century, the Midwest is still known for its lager beers. In the 1880s, for example, Milwaukee boasted more than 80 breweries. Until Schlitz moved out of town, more beer was brewed here than in any other city in the America. Now Milwaukee competes, incredibly, with the city of Portland, Oregon, for the title. The growth of small craft breweries such as Sprecher has helped restore the reputation of this once-famous brewing city, and many great lagers are brewed in this region. Indeed, for many years "microbrewed beer" was synonymous with ale, but that is changing as American brewers are rediscovering the possibilities of lagers.

ILLINOIS · INDIANA · MICHIGAN · MINNESOTA

MISSOURI · NEBRASKA · OHIO · WISCONSIN

ILLINOIS

Chicago Brewing Company

Housed in a 1920s pickle factory, the Chicago Brewing Company introduced Legacy Lager in 1990, and has gained a great reputation for producing high-quality beers. Owned and operated by the Dinehart family, the brewery got its name from Huck's Chicago Brewing Company (1847-1871), which was the country's largest brewery until it burned down in the Great Chicago Fire of 1871. Using a 40-year-old, all-copper Bavarian brewhaus imported from Kulmbach, Germany, Chicago Brewing has the capacity to produce 30,000 barrels of beer per year. 1830 N. Beasly Ct., Chicago, IL 60622, (312) 252-2739.

Chicago's Big Shoulders Porter

(og: 1.054; abw: 4.15%)

Hops: Chinook, Willamette

Malts/grains: Two-row, Caramel, Special Roast, Chocolate, Roasted Barley

Softer and less bitter than a stout, this smooth coffee-colored porter with garnet highlights has a nice burnt chocolate nose with no hops to speak of.

Chicago's Legacy Lager

(og: 1.050; abw: 3.89%)

Hops: Chinook, Mt. Hood

Malts/grains: Two-row, Munich, Caramel, plus dextrin

Bright amber in hue, with a light head that leaves some lace as it falls, this well-balanced lager has a hoppy bitterness offset by a malty, slightly sweet body. This is a full lager, enjoyed even in wintertime, with a pleasant bitter tang.

Bottled beers not photographed:

Heartland Weiss

(og: 1.046; abw: 3.75%)

Hops: Chinook

Malts/grains: Six-row, Wheat

Legacy Red Ale

(og: 1.050; abw: 3.92%)

Hops: Chinook, Willamette

Malts/grains: Two-row, Victory, Caramel

Pavichevich Brewing Company

All-natural, these beers are made in suburban Elmhurst by Ken Pavichevich, a former police officer on Chicago's South Side who spent years traveling through Europe researching great beers. Passionate about his beers (he insists on pouring for you), Pavichevich has even flown his staff to Europe to taste over 200 beers at 70 breweries. His fans are legendary—ranging from George Bush to the Soviet Red Army hockey team. In 1992, Forbes Magazine even quoted medical doctors who recommend a bottle of Baderbrau daily for its nutritional value. Ken Pavichevich proudly conforms to the German Purity Law, and is pleased to note that the German Consulate in Chicago has served Baderbrau at official functions since 1989. 383 Romans Rd., Elmhurst, IL 60126, (708) 617-5252.

Baderbräu Bock Beer

(abw: 4.6%)

Hops: 95% Czech Saaz

Malts/grains: Two-row, Six-row, Caramel, Chocolate

Fire-brewed in a copper kettle, this dark ruby-colored bock is very smooth, with a hint of coffee from the chocolate malted barley.

Baderbräu Pilsener Beer

(abw: 3.7%)

Hops: 95% Czech Saaz

Malts/grains: Two-row, Six-row, Caramel

Praised by Michael Jackson as "the best pilsner I have ever tasted in America," this light-tasting lager is clear and golden, with a full lasting head and favorable balance between the hops and malt.

INDIANA

Mishawaka Brewing Company

Home of an *Anacreontic Society*, this brewpub revived a long-standing local tradition of brewing beer that began in 1839 when a German immigrant from Detroit built a five-barrel wood fired brewhouse in Mishawaka. The pub features British dishes such as bangers 'n mash and Scotch eggs, as well as filtered beers served under pressure. They also make a Silver Hawks Pilsner Thursday Special, a European-style pilsner named after the South Bend Silver Hawks that you'll find on tap at Coveleski Stadium. 3703 N. Main St., Mishawaka, IN 46545, (219) 256-9993.

Mishawaka Brewing Company Founder's Stout

(og: 1.050; abw: 3.8%)

Hops: Perle, Willamette, Mt. Hood

Malts/grains: Two-row, Crystal, Black Patent, Roasted Barley, Black Barley

This Irish-style dry stout has an initial malt and coffee flavor brought into focus by a dry-roasted bitter finish.

Mishawaka Brewing Company
Four Horsemen Ale

(og: 1.050; abw: 3.8%)

Hops: Perle, Willamette, Mt. Hood

Malts/grains: Two-row, Crystal, Munich, Chocolate, Victory

This assertively hopped ESB has a pronounced residual maltiness and the faintest suggestion of chocolate.

Bottled beers not photographed:

Ankenbrock Weizen

(og: 1.050; abw: 3.8%)

Hops: Perle, Saaz

Malts/grains: Six-row, Malted Wheat

Hop Head Ale

(og: 1.060; abw: 4.6%)

India Pale Ale

Hops: Centennial, Cascade, Chinook

Malts/grains: Two-row, Victory, Carapils

INDIAna Pale

(og: 1.063: abw: 4.9%)

Hops: Chinook, Mt. Hood, Willamette

Malts/grains: Vienna, Victory, Carapils, Caramel

Lake Effect Pale Ale

(og: 1.052; abw: 4%)

Hops: Cascade, Perle, Willamette

Malts/grains: Two-row, Carapils

INDIANA

MICHIGAN

Frankenmuth Brewery

 Situated on the Cass River in Saginaw Valley, the town of Frankenmuth was settled in 1845 by German immigrants from Bavaria, and is still known as "Michigan's Little Bavaria." The brewery, which dates back to 1862, was almost destroyed by a devastating fire in 1987, and was resurrected when Frankenmuth Brewery was founded in 1987. True to the region's heritage, the brewery produces many beers in the Bavarian tradition. In 1996, Frankenmuth was devastated again—this time by a tornado—and is rebuilding its facility. 425 S. Main St., Frankenmuth, MI 48734, (517) 652-6183.

Frankenmuth Pilsener

(og: 1.046; abw: 3.9%)

Hops: Clusters, Perle

Malts/grains: Six-row

This tangy, possibly citrus, copper-colored lager is crisp and invigorating.

Old Detroit Amber Ale

(og: 1.055; abw: 3.95%)

Hops: Clusters, Perle

Malts/grains: Six-row, Munich, Caramel 60L, Carapils

This reddish-colored, top-fermented beer has a light hopping that accentuates the sweetness from the malts. The beer won the 1994 Can of the Year award from the Beer Can Collectors of America.

Bottled beers not photographed:

Frankenmuth Bock

(og: 1.066; abw: 5.2%)

Hops: Clusters, Perle

Malts/grains: Six-row, Munich, Caramel 60L, Black Patent, Carapils, Munich

Frankenmuth Dark

(og: 1.054; abw: 4%)

Hops: Clusters, Perle

Malts/grains: Six-row, Munich, Caramel 60L, Black Patent

Frankenmuth Oktoberfest

seasonal

(og: 1.050; abw: 3.9%)

Hops: Clusters, Perle

Malts/grains: Six-row, Munich, Carapils

Old Detroit Red Lager

(og: 1.050; abw: 3.9%)

Hops: Clusters, Perle

Malts/grains: Six-row, Munich, Caramel 60L, Carapils

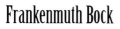

MINNESOTA

Black Moon Brewing Company

Coyote Amber Lager is the first commercial beer brewed with mesquite-roasted malt. Contract-brewed at Stroh's in St. Paul, Coyote was developed by brewmaster Joe Hertrich, a history buff who was intrigued by an ancient custom of serving beer in clay jars carved with the symbol of the coyote. P.O. Box 65383, St. Paul, MN 55165.

Coyote Amber Lager

Hops: Mt. Hood, Cascade

Malts/grains: Mesquite-roasted, Caramel, Pale

This dry-hopped (double-hopped) lager has a mild malt character and crisp clean finish.

Cold Spring Brewing Company

In 1874, a German immigrant brewer named Michael Sargi settled in Cold Spring and was delighted by the effect the bright water had on his beer. He established the Cold Spring Brewing Company, which survived prohibition by producing soda and sparkling mineral waters. The company is now owned by Beverage International and produces 50,000 barrels per year. Interestingly, over 80% of Cold Spring Brewing's sales come from mineral water and nonalcoholic beverages. They also contract-brew for many microbreweries, including San Rafael. 219 N. Red River Ave., Cold Spring, MN 56320, (612) 685-8686.

Cold Spring Honey Almond

(og: 1.044; abw: 3.6%)

Hops: Liquid hop extract

Malts/grains: Six-row

The nose is sweetly redolent of a golden thistle honey. Light-bodied, this lager is the perfect foil to hearty-flavored foods such as mushrooms. Sweet enough to be an aperitif.

Cold Spring Blackberry Bramble

(og: 1.054; abw: 4.1%)

Hops: Cascade, Willamette

Malts/grains: Six-row, Caramel 60L, plus blackberry

Well-hopped enough to stand up to the blackberry, with just a hint of berry in the finish. Perfect for poultry, fish, and summer evenings on the porch.

Bottled beers not photographed:

Cold Spring River Road Red

(og: 1.048; abw: 4.1%)

Hops: Cascade, Willamette Chinook

Malts/grains: Six-row, Caramel 60L and 80L

Cold Spring Pale Ale

(og: 1.054; abw: 4.4%)

Hops: Cascade, Willamette

Malts/grains: Six row, Caramel 60L

Summit Brewing Company

 Opened in 1986, this popular 25-barrel microbrewery in the Twin Cities features pre-war equipment brought over from a brewery in Heimertingen, Germany. 2264 University Ave., St. Paul, MN 55114, (612) 645-5029.

Summit Extra Pale Ale

(og: 1.048; abw: 3.9%)

Hops: Fuggles, Eroica, Cascade

Malts/grains: Pale, Caramel

Amber-colored with red hues, this bold ale with a pronounced hoppy flavor and distinctively fruity esters is their flagship.

Summit Great Northern Porter

(og: 1.053; abw: 4.3%)

Hops: Fuggles, Eroica, Cascade

Malts/grains: Pale, Caramel, Black Patent

This medium-bodied slightly bitter porter is very dark and rather dryish.

Bottled beers not photographed:

Heimertingen Maibock

spring seasonal

(og: 1.064; abw: 6%)

Hops: Czech Saaz, Mt. Hood

Malts/grains: Pale, Munich

Summit Dusseldorfer Style Alt Bier

fall seasonal

(og: 1.050; abw: 3.9%)

Hops: Northern Brewer, Saaz, Tettnanger

Malts/grains: Wheat, Pale, Munich, Caramel

Summit India Pale Ale

spring seasonal

(abw: 4.7%)

Hops: Kent Goldings

Malts/grains: Pale, Caramel

Summit Winter Ale

winter seasonal

(og: 1.058; abw: 4.9%)

Hops: Fuggles, Willamette, Tettnanger

Malts/grains: Pale, Caramel, Black Patent

MISSOURI

Boulevard Brewing Company

John McDonald was originally a cabinet maker who fell in love with European beers on a trip to Europe in 1980. He went on to study brewing at the Siebel Institute in Chicago, and opened Boulevard Brewing company in 1989 in a converted turn-of-the-century warehouse that was built as the laundry for the Santa Fe Railroad. Using a 1938 German-made copper kettle, the company produced 23,000 barrels of beer in 1995, selling primarily in neighboring Midwestern states. (Indeed, nearly 80% of Boulevard's beer is sold within a 50-mile radius of Kansas City.) 2501 Southwest Blvd., Kansas City, MO 64108, (816) 474-7095.

MN / MISSOURI

Boulevard Bully! Porter

(og: 1.058; abw: 4.35%)

Hops: Nuggets, Cascade, Liberty

Malts/grains: Pale, Crystal 50-60L, Chocolate 500-550L, Wheat

A dry, medium-bodied dark ale, with its roasted coffee flavor complemented by decent body and lacy head, as well as a lively hop character.

MISSOURI

Boulevard Pale Ale

(og: 1.049; abw: 3.89%)

Hops: Nugget, Cascade

Malts/grains: Pale, Carastan 30-37L, Crystal 50-60L

Boulevard's first and most popular beer, this fresh, fruity medium-bodied ale fills the mouth with a fresh floral bouquet and ends with a lasting hoppy finish.

Boulevard Tenpenny American Bitter

(og: 1.038; abw: 2.68%)

Hops: Nugget, Liberty

Malts/grains: Pale, Munich, Light Carastan 13-17L, Black 600L

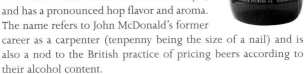

Low in alcohol, this mild refreshing ale is a rendition of the classic British bitter style, and has a pronounced hop flavor and aroma. The name refers to John McDonald's former career as a carpenter (tenpenny being the size of a nail) and is also a nod to the British practice of pricing beers according to their alcohol content.

Boulevard Wheat Beer

(og: 1.046; abw: 3.71%)

Hops: Nugget, Liberty

Malts/grains: Pale, Crystal 50-60L, Wheat

Brewed with locally-grown wheat, this American-style wheat beer is light, fruity, and refreshing with just a hint of bitter-ness—thirst-quenching on hot summer nights.

Bottled beers not photographed:

Boulevard Bob's 47

fall seasonal Munich-style lager

(og: 1.054; abw: 4.17%)

Hops: Nugget, Hersbrucker
Malts/grains: Pale, Munich, Crystal 50-60L

Boulevard Irish Ale

spring seasonal

(og: 1.054; abw: 4.21%)

Hops: Nugget, Kent Goldings
Malts/grains: Pale, Munich, Crystal 50-60L, Chocolate, Wheat

NEBRASKA

Crane River Brewpub & Cafe

You'll have to visit Lincoln to try this beer, which is available at the pub in bottles and containers of all sizes. The pub is next to Lincoln's Center for the Performing Arts, and frequented by visiting performers. (When London's Royal Philharmonic performed, a few orchestra members came by the afternoon of the show, and were wowed by the Platte Valley ESB— a taste from home they missed. They vowed to return, and during intermission that evening, 15 musicians dressed in tails ran off the stage, out the back door, and into the bar for a few quick pints before the second half. The newspaper review the next day reported that the second half of the performance was less technically precise, but brewmaster Kristina Tiebel claims, "it had more soul.") Opened in 1992, the pub is operated by Kristina and Linda Vescio, two biologists and homebrewers who attended a microbrew conference, put together a plan, and secured a loan. All beers are unfiltered. 200 N. 11th St., Lincoln, NB 68508, (402) 476-7766.

MO / NEBRASKA

Crane River Sodhouse Altbier

(og: 1.046; abw: 4%)

Hops: Hallertauer

Malts/grains: Pilsner, Munich, Vienna, Wheat, Crystal Black

Dark blonde, with a medium-light body, this altbier has a faint bitterness and rather roasty finish.

Bottled beers not photographed:

Good Life Stout

(og: 1.044: abw: 3.5%)

Hops: Bullion, Willamette

Malts/grains: Pale, Amber, Roasted Barley, Chocolate, Munich, Rolled Oats, Flaked Barley

Homestead Pale Ale

(og: 1.040; abw: 3%)

Hops: Bullion, Willamette, Cascade

Malts/grains: Pale, Crystal

Platte Valley ESB

(og: 1.040; abw: 3%)

Hops: Bullion, Willamette, Cascade

Malts/grains: Pale, Crystal

Whooping Wheat

(og: 1.042; abw: 3.5%)

Hops: Cascade, Hallertauer

Malts/grains: Pale, Malted Wheat

Zlate Pivo

(og: 1.042; abw: 3.5%)

Hops: Saaz

Malts/grains: Pale, Pilsner

OHIO

Devil Mountain Brewing Company

The Devil Mountain Brewing Company won three GABF medals its first year in business. That was in 1987 and success propelled the company to move from its 7-barrel brewhouse, a former railroad station at the foot of Mount Diablo in Walnut Creek, California to a 23-barrel warehouse up the road in Benicia. The company was eventually bought by The Seagram Beverage Company, which today contract-brews all the beer at Hudepohl-Schoenling, 1625 Central Parkway, Cincinnati, OH 45214, (513) 241-4344.

Devil Mountain Black Honey Ale

(og: 1.061; abw: 4.3%)

Hops: Liberty, Northern Brewer

Malts/grains: Pale, Caramel, Chocolate, Black, plus African black honey and New England buckwheat honey

The color of black coffee, this opaque ale has a slightly sweet profile with a somewhat bitter aftertaste.

Devil Mountain Five Malt Ale

(og: 1.053; abw: 4.2%)

Hops: Liberty, Cascade

Malts/grains: Pale, Caramel, Crystal, Chocolate, Black Patent

A well-rounded malty ale—not terribly deep or dark—that is tasty with pizza and spicy food.

Devil Mountain Railroad Gold Ale

(og: 1.048; abw: 4.1%)

Hops: Liberty, Chinook

Malts/grains: Pale, Caramel

With an easygoing mouth-feel, this light airy beer is eminently quaffable.

Great Lakes Brewing Company

In 1870, Cleveland had almost 30 breweries (most of them neighborhood joints); today there are two, this brewpub included. Some beer aficionados think it is one of the best microbreweries east of the Mississippi. The brewery is located in an 1860 former feed store that is rich in history—not only did John D. Rockefeller have his first accounting office in this building, but it later became a bar that Elliot Ness frequented (check out the bullet hole when you visit). Great Lakes Brewing was opened in 1988 by two brothers who started with a Dortmunder-style lager and, by 1995, were producing eight styles and had completed a $1 million expansion that quadrupled production capacity. 2516 Market St., Cleveland, OH 44113, (216) 771-4404.

Great Lakes Burning River Pale Ale

(abw: 4.8%)

Hops: Cascade

Malts/grains: Two-row, Crystal, Victory

With no preservatives, this medium bodied, copper colored ale is fruity and robust, with a spicy hop complexity. The beer is a tongue-in-cheek reference to a 1969 fire on the once-polluted Cuyahoga River (which flows through downtown Cleveland) that burned out of control for months.

Great Lakes Dortmunder Gold

(abw: 4.3%)

Hops: Cascade, Hallertauer

Malts/grains: Two-row Pale, Caramel

The flagship, this clear golden lager has a light hoppy flavor and pleasant aftertaste. Good with salads, chicken, and fish.

Great Lakes The Edmond Fitzgerald Porter

(abw: 4.7%)

Hops: Northern Brewer, Willamette, Cascade

Malts/grains: Two-row, Crystal, Roasted Barley, Chocolate

This smooth medium-bodied porter has a well-mannered bittersweet roasted flavor and clean dry hop finish. Good with barbecued ribs, oysters, and chocolate.

OHIO

Bottled beers not photographed:

Commodore Perry India Pale Ale

(abw: 5.7%)

Hops: Kent Goldings, Galena

Malts/grains: Two-row, Caramel

Elliot Ness

Vienna-style lager

(abw: 5%)

Hops: Hallertauer, Tettnanger

Malts/grains: Two-row, Munich, Caramel

Moon Dog Ale

(abw: 4%)

Hops: Northern Brewer, Kent Goldings

Malts/grains: Two-row, Crystal, Wheat, plus dextrin

Oktoberfest

(abw: 5%)

Hops: Hallertauer, Liberty

Malts/grains: Two-row Pale, Caramel

Rockefeller Bock

(abw: 5.3%)

Hops: Tettnanger, Hallertauer

Malts/grains: Two-row Pale, Caramel, Chocolate

OHIO

Hudepohl-Schoenling Brewery

Back in 1933, when Edward Schoenling went down to Bruckmann's Brewery to buy beer after the repeal of prohibition and had to wait in a line a thousand feet long, he realized there was a demand for beer. He eventually opened a brewery, and in 1986, his heirs merged the brewery with the 101-year-old Hudepohl Brewing Company, also in Cincinnati. Though not a microbrewery (Hudepohl-Schoenling is the 10th largest brewery in the United States), the brewery has a place in the annals of craft brewing. The Hudepohl brewery not only first brewed Little Kings Cream Ale in 1958, whose success fueled the growth of the brewery from a small regional brewer to a nationally-known supplier, distributing to 44 states but, in 1983, brought back Christian Moerlein, a label that once belonged to Cincinnati's largest brewery, and was the first American beer to pass the German Purity Law. 1625 Central Parkway, Cincinnati, OH 45214, (513) 241-4344.

Little Kings Cream Ale

(og: 1.053; abw: 4.4%)

Hops: Hallertauer

Malts/grains: Six-row, Robust, Azure Excel, plus corn grits, corn syrup

This lager-ale hybrid strives to approach the body and flavor of an ale mellowed with the hop bite of a lager. Straw-colored, the beer's soft creamy taste is light and fleeting, with thirst-quenching appeal. Note the unique 7-ounce bottle.

Morlein's Cincinnati Select Lager Beer

(og: 1.048; abw: 3.8%)

Hops: Clusters, Mt. Hood, Saaz

Malts/grains: Two-row Harrington, Caramel

Light on flavor, this uncomplicated some-what sweet lager is brewed with no additives. Refreshing with pizza, Mexican foods, hot dogs, and especially after lawn-mowing.

OHIO

Bottled beers not photographed:

Christian Moerlein Bock

(og: 1.049; abw: 4%)

Hops: Clusters, Mt. Hood

Malts/grains: Two-row Harrington, Caramel, Black Patent

Hudy Delight

(og: 1.030; abw: 2.95%)

Hops: Clusters, Cascade

Malts/grains: Six-row, plus corn syrup

Little Kings Ice Cream Ale

(og: 1.058; abw: 4.9%)

Hops: Hallertauer

Malts/grains: Six-row, Robust, Azure, plus corn grits, corn syrup

Little Kings Red

(og: 1.052; abw: 4.2%)

Hops: Cascade, Mt. Hood

Malts/grains: Two-row Harrington, Caramel, Chocolate

WISCONSIN

Appleton Brewing Company

In the heart of Wisconsin, this microbrewery and attached Mexican restaurant (Dos Bandidos) are situated in a building that was the home of the Muench Brewery in the 1850s. Incorporated in 1989, Appleton Brewing company experiments with many styles of beer, bottling them with terrific silk-screened labels. (They are proud to be the smallest brewery, in the U.S. to print their own labels.) Unpasteurized, Adler Brau beers have a strong following in northeast Wisconsin. 1004 Old Oneida St., Appleton, WI 54915, (414) 731-3322.

Adler Brau Oatmeal Stout

(og: 1.050; abw: 5%)

Hops: Willamette

Malts/grains: Six-row, Two-row, Flaked Oats, Roasted Barley, Caramel 60L, Black Patent flour

Brewed with oatmeal for a generous mouth-feel and foam quality, this rich roasted stout has a bitter chocolate taste and distinct smokiness.

Adler Brau Mosquito Pilsner

(og: 1.050; abw: 5.4%)

Hops: Hallertauer, Saaz

Malts/grains: Six-row, Two-row, Wheat, Caramel 20L, Carapils

The bartender's favorite, this golden lager has a light floral aroma and astringent hop flavor.

Adler Brau Tailgate Amber

(og: 1.052; abw: 5.5%)

Hops: Northern Brewer, Hallertauer, Cascade

Malts/grains: Six-row, Two-row, Munich, Caramel 20L and 60L, Chocolate

A full-bodied, nicely-hopped lager with a distinct taste and slight bitterness.

WISCONSIN

Bottled beers not photographed:

Classic Porter

(og: 1.055)

Hops: Northern Brewer, Willamette

Malts/grains: Six-row, Two-row, Munich, Caramel 40L, Chocolate

Erich Weiss Beer

(og: 1.054)

Hops: Northern Brewer, Hallertauer, Cascade

Malts/grains: Wheat, Two-row, Munich

Marquette Export Lager

(og: 1.055)

Hops: Northern Brewer, Hallertauer, Willamette, Cascade

Malts/grains: Two-row, Wheat, Caramel 40L

Capital Brewery Company

Known for its high-quality German-style beers, Capital Brewery began in 1986 in a former egg processing plant (where the cold storage areas for poultry products with two-foot-thick walls served as perfect insulators). Most of the beers are brewed in accordance with the German Purity Law, and there is a beer garden (complete with hop bines) where beer can be sampled. Capital currently brews 13,500 barrels per year, which are available in nine Midwestern states. 7734 Terrance Ave., Middletown, WI 53562, (608) 836-7100.

Winterfest Garten Bräu

(og: 1.058; abw: 4.7%)

Hops: Spalt

Malts/grains: Brewer's, Caramel

This beefed-up amber-style seasonal beer is mildly bitter, with a distinct hop flavor that laces through the malt.

Wisconsin Amber Garten Bräu

(og: 1.051; abw: 4.2%)

Hops: Cascade, Mt. Hood

Malts/grains: Brewers, Imported Specialty

Loosely based on the Vienna style, this copper-colored beer has a fine lasting head, with modest hopping.

Bottled beers not photographed:

Dark Garten Bräu

(og: 1.051; abw: 4.2)

Hops: Clusters, Saaz, Northern Brewer

Malts/grains: Carapils, Caramel, Black Patent

WISCONSIN

Liam Mahoney's Brown Ale

(og: 1.050; abw: 4.1%)

Hops: Fuggles, Brewer's Gold

Malts/grains: Crystal

Special Garten Bräu

pilsner

(og: 1.045; abw: 3.9%)

Hops: Clusters, Saaz, Northern Brewer

Malts/grains: Carapils, Munich, Caramel

Wild Rice Garten Bräu

(og: 1.050; abw: 4.2%)

Hops: Clusters, Cascade, Willamette, Northern Brewer

Malts/grains: Ecimalt, Wild Rice

Cherryland Brewing Company

Located in Door County, this brewpub was established in a 19th-century railroad station in 1988 by homebrewers Mark Field and Tom Alberts. Specializing in lagers, their beers quickly became popular and have received numerous awards. Cherryland still brews some beer on the premises, and also contracts with Dubuque Brewing Company in Iowa. 341 N. 3rd Ave., Sturgeon Bay, WI 54235, (414) 743-1945.

Cherry Rail

(og: 1.044; abw: 4%)

Hops: Cascade

Malts/grains: Two-row Pale, plus cherry juice

This light lager is brewed with cherry juice to give a slight fruity tart taste that overrides the malt flavor. Try it with crepes suzette.

Golden Rail

(og: 1.050; abw: 4.8%)

Hops: Tettnanger

Malts/grains: Two-row Pale, Crystal, Munich

This Vienna-style amber has a general roasted malt flavor that is accentuated by hop notes.

Bottled beers not photographed:

Apple Bach

(og: 1.052; abw: 5%)

Hops: Cascade, Tettnanger

Malts/grains: Crystal Roast

Door County Weiss

(og: 1.042; abw: 3.6%)

Hops: Perle, Cascade

Malts/grains: Pale, Crystal, Malted Wheat

Raspberry Bier

(og: 1.042; abw: 3.7%)

Hops: Cascade

Malts/grains: Two-row Pale, plus raspberry juice

Silver Rail

pilsner

(og: 1.046; abw: 4.2%)

Hops: Hallertauer

Malts/grains: Two-row Pale

Jacob Leinenkugel Brewing Company

One of the oldest continuously operating breweries in Wisconsin, Leinenkugel was bought by Miller Brewing in 1988. The brewery—which has developed a cult following in the Wisconsin Northwoods—is still run by Jake Leinenkugel and his family, who brew the beer according to the original recipes. The beer is now being shipped to 31 states. 1-3 Jefferson Ave., Chippewa Falls, WI 54729, (715) 723-5558.

Leinenkugel's Honey Weiss Bier

(og: 1.175; abw; 3.85%)

Hops: Yakima Valley

Malts/grains: Pale, Wheat

A mild, summery, straightforward beer brewed with honey, yielding a faint hint of honey in the palate, but no aroma.

Leinenkugel's Red Lager

(og: 1.175; abw: 3.85%)

Hops: Clusters, Mt. Hood

Malts/grains: Six-row Pale, Two-row Pale, Caramel, Carapils

With a deep copper-red color, this beer (known locally as "Leinie's") looks like an ale, but drinks like a lager. A handsome beer, lighter than it looks, with a middle-of-the-road malty aroma and hop bitterness.

Lakefront Brewery

This small brewery in the tradition of early Milwaukee breweries is a labor of love. Located in a former bakery in the Riverwood district of Milwaukee, it was founded in 1987 by Russell and Jim Klisch, homebrewing brothers who fashioned brew equipment from scavenged junkyard parts and tools. The brewery produced 60 barrels the first year, and the brothers still celebrate the anniversary date of their first sale at the pub that bought their beer. The labels are designed by a local homebrewing artist, and often reflect Milwaukee's diverse architectural heritage. By 1994, Lakefront was producing 1,600 barrels per year. 818A E. Chambers St., Milwaukee, WI 53212, (414) 372-8800.

Lakefront Pumpkin Lager Beer

fall seasonal

(og: 1.055; abw: 5.8%)

Hops: Clusters

Malts/grains: Two-row Malted Barley, Crystal, Munich, Carapils

This delicious lager is brewed with pumpkin that is added to the mash, while the salt, cinnamon, and nutmeg are added during the boil. Lightly hopped and rather malty, it reminds me of pumpkin pie.

Riverwest Stein Beer

(og: 1.060; abw: 5.8%)

Hops: Mt. Hood, Cascade

Malts/grains: Two-row Malted Barley, Crystal, Roasted Barley

This rich, amber-colored all-malt beer has a hint of caramel, with the roasted barley providing a subtle toasted background. The hoppy finish cuts through the malty character, leaving a clean palate.

Bottled beers not photographed:

Cream City Pale Ale

(og: 1.060; abw: 5.8%)

Hops: Clusters, Cascade

Malts/grains: Two-row Malted Barley, Caramel, Munich, Carapils

Eastside Dark

(og: 1.060; abw: 5.8%)

Hops: Mt. Hood

Malts/grains: Two-row Malted Barley

Klisch Pilsner

(og: 1.060; abw: 5.8%)

Hops: Mt. Hood

Malts/grains: Two-row Malted Barley

Sprecher Brewing Company

Sprecher was founded in 1985 by Randal Sprecher, a former brewing supervisor at Pabst Brewing Company who wanted to brew distinctive beers that would restore the tradition of regional beers to this famous brewing city. Brewing in a former car elevator factory, Sprecher produces excellent European and traditional-style beers. 701 W. Glendale Ave., Milwaukee, WI 53209, (414) 964-2739.

Sprecher Belgian Style Ale

fall seasonal

(og: 1.075; abw: 7-8%)

Hops: Tettnanger, Mt. Hood, Willamette

Malts/grains: Two-row Pale, Vienna, Munich, plus dextrin

Extra-long aging lends this terrific Belgian ale a silky lingering malt finish and characteristic fruit bouquet that hints of apples. A darkish ale with a firm head, it is faintly sweet due to the addition of candy sugar.

Sprecher Black Bavarian

(og: 1.060; abw: 4.8-5%)

Hops: Cascade, Mt. Hood, Tettnanger, Chinook

Malts/grains: Two-row Pale, Caramel, Black Patent

Almost black in color, this robust Bavarian-style lager has a complex malt taste, creamy head and aromas of caramel and coffee. Delicious with spicy foods, it's pretty light tasting for a dark beer.

Bottled beers not photographed:

Hefe Weiss

(og: 1.044: abw: 3.5%)

Hops: Cascade, Mt. Hood, Tettnanger

Malts/grains: Two-row Pale, Wheat Malt, Carapils

Special Amber

(og: 1.052; abw: 4.2%)

Hops: Cascade, Mt. Hood, Tettnanger

Malts/grains: Two-row Pale, Carapils, Caramel

WISCONSIN

SOUTH & SOUTHEAST

Perhaps not surprisingly, the hot and humid South and Southeast inspire relatively high proportions of lagers and light ales. Though newer than many microbreweries in the West and Midwest, several of these Southern companies are developing unique products that rank highly among their peers.

ALABAMA ❦ ARKANSAS ❦ FLORIDA ❦ GEORGIA

KENTUCKY ❦ LOUISIANA ❦ TEXAS ❦ WASHINGTON D.C.

ALABAMA

Birmingham Brewing Company

 Birmingham is known for its limestone deposits and hard water, which Ben Hogan finds ideal for brewing beer. The Birmingham Brewing Company was started in 1992 in a converted 1930s warehouse, and is the first brewery in the region since prohibition. 3118 Third Ave. S., Birmingham, AL 35233, (205) 326-6677.

Red Mountain Golden Lager

(og: 1.045; abw: 4.2%)

Hops: Noble Hops

Malts/grains: Two-row

With a muted reddish-golden color, this lager is good and quaffable, though the finish is quite light.

Red Mountain Red Ale

(og: 1.050; abw: 4.9%)

Hops: Willamette, Cascade

Malts/grains: Two-row Pale, Roasted Barley

A deep copper-colored ale with a respectable malt character, this beer received an honorable mention at the GABF in 1995.

Bottled beers not photographed:

Red Mountain Golden Ale

(og: 1.046)

Hops: Cascade

Malts/grains: Two-row Pale

Red Mountain Wheat Beer

(og: 1.050; abw: 3.9%)

Hops: Willamette, Clusters

Malts/grains: Pale, Crystal, Roasted Barley

ARKANSAS

Weidman's Brew Pub

This brewpub is located in a beautiful stone building that was built as a brewery in 1848, when Fort Smith was a military post and the Indian territory was within hailing distance across the Arkansas River. Listed on the National Historic Register, the building was constructed with hand-hewn timbers that still show the axe marks a hundred and fifty years later. (Interestingly, a 1996 tornado only affected the construction added in the twentieth century.) Run by the Weidman family since 1992, this brewery bottles four beers, including a watermelon-flavored ale that's a nod to Hope, Arkansas, the melon capital of the world. 422 North 3rd Street, Fort Smith, AK 72901, (501) 782-9898.

Naked Nut Brown Ale

(og: 1.042; abw: 3.7%)

Malts/grains: Two-row, Caramel, Roasted Barley, Chocolate

A dense dark-colored brown that is almost opaque, this slightly yeasty ale is lighter in taste than its rich, creamy mouth-feel leads you to believe.

Rope Swing Red Ale

(og: 1.036; abw: 3.2%)

Malts/grains: Two-row, Caramel

Yeasty and full of promise, this very drinkable red-tinged ale has a thick head and good bouquet, with a nice tang and flavor.

Bottled beers not photographed:

Danny Boy Stout

(og: 1.050; abw: 4.1%)

Malts/grains: Two-row, Caramel, Chocolate, Roasted Barley, Black Barley

H²O Melon Ale

(og: 1.047; abw: 4%)

FLORIDA

Florida Beer Brands

In 1988, sportswear manufacturer Bill Burrer decided that Florida needed a regional beer, and so he came up with Growlin' Gator. Interested in American history, he next introduced Warrior Beer, whose label depicted famous Indian warriors. The label didn't go over well with the Bureau of Alcohol, Firearms, and Tobacco, so Burrer moved on to "Old West" personalities with his amber beer, which sports 20 labels depicting personalities ranging from Calamity Jane to Wild Bill Hickok. He also makes Gator Lager (which is packaged under the label Gator Lager Brewing Company). His beers are contract-brewed at the August Schell Brewing Company. Corporate office: P.O. Box 561357, Orlando, FL 32856, (407) 423-3929.

AK / FLORIDA

Famous Old West Etta Place Amber Beer

(og: 1.050; abw: 4%)

Hops: Cascade, Mt. Hood

Malts/grains: Two-row Pale, Caramel

A quick-draw amber with a characteristic hint of chocolate from the roasted grains, but mostly an effervescent light-tasting beer.

Famous Old West John Wesley Hardin Amber Beer

(og: 1.050; abw: 4%)

Hops: Cascade, Mt. Hood

Malts/grains: Two-row Pale, Caramel

Identical to Famous Old West Etta Place Amber Beer (above), with a different label.

Growlin' Gator Lager

(og: 1.045; abw: 4.5%)

Hops: Yakima, Saaz

Malts/grains: Two-row Pale, plus corn syrup

A decent, light golden lager in the tradition of American lawn-mowing and canoe-sex beers.

Bottled beers not photographed:

Flying Aces Light Beer

(abw: 3.7%)

Hops: Northwest Blend

Malts/grains: Six-row

Gator Light

(og: 1.040; abw: 3.2%)

Hops: Northwest Variety

Malts/grains: Six-row

FLORIDA

GEORGIA

Wild Boar Brewing Company

In 1989, Atlanta homebrewers Rob Nelson and Bob Clark started brewing Wild Boar Special Amber, and arranged to have it contract-brewed at the Dubuque Brewing Company in Iowa. In the early 1990s Dubuque Brewing had financial problems, and the upshot was that Nelson and Clark formed a partnership with Dubuque, which is currently brewing 35,000 barrels per year. The beer is still brewed in Iowa, but Nelson and Clark remain in Atlanta. Corporate office: P.O. Box 8239, Atlanta, GA 30306, (404) 633-0924.

Wild Boar Special Amber

(og: 1.052; abw: 3.8%)

Hops: Cascade, Tettnanger

Malts/grains: Caramel, Pale

This Vienna-style amber is slightly cloudy, with a malty sweetness, playful hoppy flavor, and fading hop finish.

Wild Boar Wild Wheat

(og: 1.052; abw: 3.9%)

Hops: Tettnanger

Malts/grains: Pale, Wheat

Recently renamed Wild Boar Hefeweizen, this cloudy golden ale has a crisp wheat taste and slightly sweet, pleasant aftertaste. Brewed with 50% wheat. Inspired by a Bavarian weiss.

GEORGIA

Bottled beers not photographed:

Wild Boar Black Forest Wheat

dunkelweizen

Malts/grains: Chocolate, Wheat, plus a cherry purée

Wild Boar Classic Pilsner

(og: 1.049; abw: 3.8%)

Hops: Saaz

Malts/grains: Carapils, Pale

Wild Boar Wild Winter

winter seasonal

(og: 1.052; abw: 3.8%)

Hops: Cascade

Malts/grains: Chocolate, Caramel

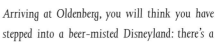

KENTUCKY

Oldenberg Brewery

Arriving at Oldenberg, you will think you have stepped into a beer-misted Disneyland: there's a beer garden, the "Great Hall" (cozy dining for 650 people), a retail shop, and a breweriana museum on the eight-acre site. Call on the telephone, and the automated voice instructs you to "press two for stock offerings." Not a sleepy place. Still, the beers are very good. The brewery opened in 1987 and is a popular destination five miles south of Cincinnati (an area with a rich tradition of German immigrants and lager breweries). Twice a year the brewery hosts "Beer Camp," a fun-filled weekend that includes beer tastings, demonstrations, and lectures. They feature many styles on tap. 400 Buttermilk Pike, Fort Mitchell, KY 41017, (606) 341-7223.

GA / KENTUCKY

Oldenberg Holy Grail Nut Brown Ale

(og: 1.050; abw: 4.5%)

Hops: Northern Brewer, Fuggles, Willamette

Malts/grains: Two-row, Munich, Chocolate, Vienna, Victory, plus dextrin

With a soft smooth head, this medium-bodied brown ale has a characteristic malty overtone, with a subtle nutty flavor and sharp aftertaste.

Oldenberg Premium Verum Amber

(og: 1.046; abw: 3.8%)

Hops: Saaz, Cascade

Malts/grains: Pale, Two-row, Munich, Black Malt, plus dextrin

This uncomplicated German lager is 14-karat gold in color, with a light body and mellow taste. A pleasing, straightforward beer.

LOUISIANA

Abita Brewing Company

Abita Brewing Company began bottling beer in 1989 in this old spa-town north of New Orleans, and has more than doubled its sales each year since. Cold-filtered and unpasteurized, these brewers use Abita spring water once prized by the Choctaw Indians. The brewery now produces 35,000 barrels per year, and can be found in most restaurants in New Orleans. The name is derived from New-castle Brown Ale, which is known throughout England as "the dog" because Newcastle coal miners would decline their wives' invitation to share a cup of tea after work, demurring that they needed to "walk the dog." Anyone passing the pubs in Newcastle could tell by the dogs tied up outside how popular the brown ale had become. Following tradition, many of Abita's beers are introduced at Carnival. 100 Leveson, Abita Springs, LA 70420, (504) 893-3143.

Abita Amber

(og: 1.044; abw: 4%)

Hops: Perle, Crystal

Malts/grains: Caramel

Startlingly hoppy up front, this faintly fizzy amber is followed up with a smooth roasty flavor that has just a hint of caramel.

Abita Turbodog

(og: 1.056; abw: 4.9%)

Hops: Willamette

Malts/grains: Pale, Caramel, Chocolate

A deep reddish-brown, this brown ale is surprisingly dry, and almost crisp in the finish. Eminently quaffable, it has a roasty chocolate aroma, with a light body and coarse short-lived head. It began as a specialty ale, but became so popular that it's now one of Abita's standard brews.

Bottled beers not photographed:

Abita Bock

(og: 1.054; abw: 4.9%)

Hops: Yakima Perle

Malts/grains: British Two-row, Caramel

Abita Golden

(og: 1.040; abw: 4.2%)

Hops: Mt. Hood

Malts/grains: English Lager

Abita Wheat

summer seasonal

(og: 1.040; abw: 3.8%)

Hops: Mt. Hood

Fall Fest

fall seasonal Octoberfest

(og: 1.050; abw: 4.9%)

Hops: German Hersbrucker

Malts/grains: Two-row Pale, Crystal, Chocolate

Dixie Brewing Company

Founded in 1907, this brewery survived prohibition by making ice cream and near beer, and still brews its beers in the original cypress wood tanks. (The brewery is also still located at its original spot on Tulane Avenue, behind the antique iron gates of the brewhouse.) While not technically a microbrewery (capacity is 300,000 barrels per year), Dixie's Voodoo Lager is a cult favorite, especially since the state of Texas tried to ban it five years ago because of the implied voodoo connection. (The state of Louisiana retaliated by threatening to ban Lone Star, and the feud was abandoned.) 2401 Tulane Ave., New Orleans, LA 70119, (504) 822-8711.

Dixie Blackened Voodoo Lager

(abw: 4.95%)

Hops: Mt. Hood, Cascade

Malts/grains: Black Patent, Chocolate, Two-row, Six-row, Caramel, Louisiana Rice

Styled after a German dark lager, this 100% malt beer derives its unique taste from the addition of Louisiana rice. While once dubbed a "good canoe-sex beer," it's also a "Big Easy" beer, swell to be drunk in long thirsty gulps—and irresistible with the heavily spiced foods of Creole and Cajun cuisines.

LOUISIANA

Dixie Jazz Amber Light Beer

(abw: 4.12%)

Hops: Cascade, Clusters

Malts/grains: American Barley, Louisiana Rice

Formulated by Dr. Joseph Owades (father of light beer), this good-time beer is crisper and smoother than most light beers, benefited perhaps by the cypress vats and Louisiana rice.

Bottled beers not photographed:

Dixie Crimson Voodoo Ale

red ale

(abw: 3.96%)

Hops: Cascade, Mt. Hood

Malts/grains: Caramel, Chocolate

TEXAS

Celis Brewery

At 14, Pierre Celis was working at a Belgian brewery in Hoegaarden, learning the secret of making witbier, which had been brewed in the village since 1543. By the late 1950s, however, Europeans craved Pilsner lagers, the brewery closed, and Celis ended up a milkman. Celis continued making white beer in his dad's barn and, in 1966, opened a brewery. Largely credited with resurrecting the white beer style in Belgium, Celis sold the brewery to a Belgian beer conglomerate in 1990 and moved to America. Claiming he liked the water (the lime content of which reminded him of Hoegaarden), the central shipping location, and the fact that he could understand slow-talking Texans, Celis settled in Texas, opening the Celis Brewery in 1992. His beers quickly became a hit. By 1994, Celis was shipping 15,000 barrels to 30 states. In 1995, he disappointed many fans by selling a majority interest of the brewery to Miller Brewing Company, which he claims will enable the brewery to increase production and distribution. 2431 Forbes Dr., Austin, TX 78754, (512) 835-0884.

Celis Raspberry

(og: 1.048; abw: 3.9%)

Hops: Willamette, Goldings

Malts/grains: Barley Wheat, Raw Texas Wheat, plus raspberry juice

Fermented with raspberry juice, this wheat beer is true to its Belgian-style fruit beer heritage, with a strong fruity aroma followed up by a tart raspberry flavor.

Celis White

(og: 1.048; abw: 3.9%)

Hops: Willamette, Cascade

Malts/grains: Raw Texas Winter Wheat, Barley

The Celis flagship, this wonderful wheat beer is spiced with Curaçao, orange peel, and coriander, producing a mild spicy fragrance and lush clove-like flavor and citric aftertaste. Foamy, effervescent, and thirst-quenching, it has a cloudy yellowish-white color and slightly sweet-tart taste, perfect for summer or as a dessert drink.

Bottled beers not photographed:

Celis Golden

pilsner

(og: 1.049; abw: 3.9%)

Hops: Saaz

Malts/grains: Pale Barley

Celis Grand Cru

(og: 1.080; abw: 7%)

Hops: Saaz, Cascade

Malts/grains: Pale Barley

TEXAS

Celis Pale Bock

(og: 1.050; abw: 3.9%)

Hops: Saaz, Willamette, Cascade

Malts/grains: Caramel

Note: Celis Pale Bock is actually a pale ale, but antiquated Texas law reserves the term "ale" for beer in excess of 5% alcohol.

Hill Country Brewing Company

Hailing from L.B.J. country just outside Austin, this brewery began production in the fall of 1993 as an all-volunteer operation. Using a bottling line from the 1940s, the company produces several styles of unpasteurized hand-crafted beer named after local natural landmarks. A portion of the proceeds goes to the Hill Country Foundation, which preserves the flora and fauna of the Texas hill country. 730 Shady Ln., Austin, TX 78702, (512) 385-9111.

Balcones Fault Pale Malt

(og: 1.045; abw: 3.7%)

Hops: Fuggles, Kent Goldings

Malts/grains: British Two-row, Belgian Caravienne, Belgian Carapils, Wheat

Brewed with English ale yeast grown at the brewery, this light English bitter has a slightly malty Vienna character and traditional bitter taste. The Balcones Fault runs through central Texas, separating the hill country from eastern farm land.

TEXAS

Balcones Fault Red Granite

(og: 1.045; abw: 3.7%)

Hops: Fuggles

Malts/grains: British Two-row, Crystal, Caravienne, Belgian Chocolate, Wheat

An English-style brown ale with a malty, smooth taste and medium body. The label depicts the Red Mountain near Llano, Texas.

Olde Heurich Brewing Company

Christian Heurich was a 19th-century brewer in Washington whose beers received many awards, including a silver medal for excellence at the 1900 Paris World Exposition. When the company closed in 1956, the family donated a portion of the brewery's land for the construction of the John F. Kennedy Center for the Performing Arts. In 1986, Gary Heurich resurrected his grandfather's recipes and established the Olde Heurich Brewing Company. Beers are contract-brewed. 1111 34th St. N. W., Washington, D.C. 20007, (202) 333-2313.

Heurich's Foggy Bottom Ale

Hops: Cascade, Tettnanger, Hallertauer

Malts/grains: Pale, Caramel

Dry-hopped, this spicy brew is fermented at relatively high temperatures, meaning that it can be enjoyed at cellar temperature.

Olde Heurich Maerzen Beer

Hops: Saaz, Tettnanger, Cascade

Malts/grains: Pale, Caramel

This cloudy amber is produced in the traditional German style. Twice selected as one of the country's top ten beers by the Great American Beer Festival, it's a sweet, smooth, mildly fruity brew with a clean hoppy aftertaste.

NORTHEAST

The American microbrewery beer movement began in the Northeast with the colonists, and Philadelphia (which had 94 breweries in 1879) was the nation's beer capital for many years. Today, many microbreweries in the Northeast are rediscovering this tradition, serving ales in the British style at establishments ranging from Geary's in Portland to Massachusetts Bay Brewing in Boston.

CONNECTICUT | DELAWARE | MAINE | MARYLAND

MASSACHUSETTS | NEW YORK | PENNSYLVANIA | VERMONT

CONNECTICUT

New England Brewing Company

Named after a turn-of-the-century brewery, the New England Brewing Company opened in 1989. In the last decade, they've gained a solid reputation throughout New England for producing good British-style beers, and in 1995 moved to a remodeled 22,000-square-foot building near the Maritime Center. 13 Marshall St., Norwalk, CT 06852, (203) 866-1339.

New England Atlantic Amber

(og: 1.048)

Hops: Northern Brewer, Yakima Cascade, Saaz

Malts/grains: Pale, Crystal

The company's flagship, this steam beer is fairly light in body, with a comely roasted malt flavor, a thick head, an almost sweet note, and an honest hop finish.

New England Oatmeal Stout

(og: 1.052)

Hops: Northern Brewer, Tettnanger

Malts/grains: Pale, Roasted Barley

A full, heavy stout that is dry and bitter. Good with grilled steak or strong cheeses.

Bottled beers not photographed:

American Wheat

(og: 1.050)

Hops: Northern Brewer, Yakima Cascade, Tettnanger

Malts/grains: Pale, Wheat

Gold Stock Ale

(og: 1.044)

Hops: Perle, Hallertauer, Hersbrucker, Northern Brewer, Cascade, Tettnanger, Saaz

Malts/grains: Pale, Caramel

Holiday Ale

(og: 1.054)

Hops: Perle

Malts/grains: Pale, Wheat, Munich, Chocolate, Crystal

Light Lager

(og: 1.034)

Hops: Perle, Hallertauer, Hersbrucker, Saaz

Malts/grains: Two-row Pale

New Haven Brewing Company

Just down the street from Yale University, this popular 12,000-barrel brewery opened in 1989 in an 18th-century building on the Mill River that formerly was a steamship authority building. Mr. Mike's Light Ale was intended originally as a wheat-based ale, before wheat beers were popular. 458 Grand Ave., New Haven, CT 06513, (203) 772-2739.

Blackwell Stout

(og: 1.051; abw: 4.8%)

Hops: Northern Brewer, Cascade

Malts/grains: Munich, Crystal, Wheat, Flaked Barley, Carapils

A dark, smooth, relatively still beer, with little head, and somewhat light-tasting for a stout. Named after the brewery's mascot.

CONNECTICUT

Elm City

(og: 1.047; abw: 4%)

Hops: Northern Brewer, Willamette, Hallertauer

Malts/grains: Two-row, English Crystal, Roasted Barley

Similar to a Scottish mild ale, this sweet, almost nutty amber-colored brew is lightly carbonated. A good beginner for Bud drinkers looking to try a microbrew.

Mr. Mike's Light Ale

Hops: Hallertauer

Malts/grains: Two-row Canadian, American Wheat

Arguably the first microbrewed light beer, this sweet, mild ale has a light body and color.

DELAWARE

Blue Hen Brewing Company

Contract-brewed by the Lion Brewery in Wilkes-Barre, Pennsylvania, this brewery is named after Delaware's revolutionary soldiers who carried gamecocks with them, earning the title, "The Fighting Blue Hens." Corporate office: P.O. Box 707, Newark, DE 16714-7077, (302) 737-8375.

Blue Hen Black & Tan

(og: 1.051; abw: 4.1%)

This beer is a blend of a lager beer and a porter, with the lager lending a bubbly mouth-feel that is somewhat unexpected in a dark beer. Of medium body, the beer has a hint of toffee, and a rapidly disappearing head.

Blue Hen Lager Beer

(og: 1.047; abw: 3.9%)

Hops: Mt. Hood, Cascade, Czech Saaz, Hallertauer Hersbrucker

Malts/grains: Six-row, Two-row

A flowery, complex, lightly hopped beer that won a silver medal in the 1994 World Beer Championships.

Bottled beers not photographed:

Blue Hen Porter

(og: 1.056; abw: 4.5%)

Hops: Cascade, Kent Goldings

Malts/grains: Six-row, Two-row Pale, Caramel, Chocolate

MAINE

Atlantic Brewing Company

Atlantic Brewing grew out of the Lompoc Cafe (named after a bar in W. C. Field's The Bank Dick) when owner Dough Maffucci decided he wanted to add a brewery to his bar so sent his cook to Canada to learn how to brew beer. The brewery (and restaurant) are open from May through October on the island of Mount Desert in northern Maine. 30 Rodick St., Bar Harbor, ME 04609, (207) 288-9513.

Lompoc's Bar Harbor Blueberry Ale

(og: 1.052; abw: 4.16%)

Hops: Willamette

Malts/grains: Pale, Munich, plus blueberries

This mildly-hopped light brown ale is brewed with 400 pounds of Maine wild blueberries, lending it a subtle blueberry aroma and flavor.

Lompoc's Ginger Wheat

(og: 1.056; abw: 4.57%)

Hops: Willamette

Malts/grains: Pale, Munich, plus gingerroot

A light-bodied barley and wheat beer brewed with fresh gingerroot for a quaffable summer brew.

Bottled beers not photographed:

Bar Harbor Real Ale

(og: 1.048; abw: 4.68%)

Hops: Willamette

Malts/grains: Crystal, Black Patent, Pale Barley

Coal Porter

(og: 1.050; abw: 4.94%)

Hops: Willamette, Chinook

Malts/grains: Roasted Barley, Pale Barley

Lompoc's Pale Ale

(og: 1.048; abw: 4.94%)

Hops: Chinook, Perle

Malts/grains: Pale, Munich, Barley

MAINE

Bar Harbor Brewing Company

 On Mount Desert Island, Tod and Suzi Foster bottle-condition unfiltered ales in a tiny brewery that adjoins their house. They offer tastings of the state's smallest brewery by appointment. 22 Forest St., Bar Harbor, ME 04609, (207) 288-4592.

Cadillac Mtn. Stout

(og: 1.075)

Hops: Cascade, Willamette, Clusters

Malts/grains: British Chocolate, Roasted Barley, Pale, Mild, Crystal

This hearty Imperial stout has a rounded roasty flavor, with a slight sweetness and smooth taste. Named after one of Mount Desert's natural attractions.

Thunder Hole Ale

(og: 1.060)

Hops: Cascade, Willamette, Clusters

Malts/grains: British Pale, Mild, Crystal, Chocolate

A full-bodied malty brown ale with a lasting head and suggestion of chocolate. Good with steak or lamb.

Bottled beers not photographed:

Bar Harbor Ginger Mild Brew

(og: 1.036)

Hops: Cascade, Willamette, Clusters

Malts/grains: British Pale, Mild, Crystal, Chocolate, plus fresh gingerroot

MAINE

Harbor Lighthouse Ale

(og: 1.036)

Hops: Cascade, Willamette, Clusters

Malts/grains: British Pale, Mild, Crystal, Chocolate

D. L. Geary Brewing Company

 David Geary traveled to Scotland and England to learn the art of brewing before opening Maine's first brewery in the early 1980s with his wife Karen. Geary's Pale Ale entered the market in 1986, and has been a hit ever since. Now available in 15 states. 38 Evergreen Dr., Portland, ME 04103, (207) 878-2337.

Geary's Hampshire Special Ale

winter seasonal

(og: 1.070; abw: 7%)

Hops: Cascade, Mt. Hood, Kent Goldings

Malts/grains: Two-row English Pale, Crystal, Chocolate

With a long finish, this ale has a generous nutty malt flavor and assertive hoppiness.

Geary's Pale Ale

(og: 1.047; abw: 4.5%)

Hops: Cascade, Mt. Hood, Tettnanger, Fuggles

Malts/grains: Two-row English Pale, Crystal, Chocolate

Made with imported Hampshire yeast, this English-style ale is dry, clean, and crisp, with a late hop taste.

MAINE

Bottled beers not photographed:

Geary's London Porter

(og: 1.045; abw: 4.2%)

Hops: Cascade, Willamette, Goldings

Malts/grains: Two-row English Pale, Crystal, Chocolate, Black Patent

Kennebunkport Brewing Company

Founded in 1992 on the site of three historic shipyards where four-masted schooners were built, the Kennebunkport Brewing Company is a small brewery and pub on the harbor. Owned by the Shipyard Brewing Company, the brewery is now part of Shipyard's partnership with Miller Brewing, with Kennebunkport supplying beer to the pub (which is not owned by Miller) and making a few seasonal beers such as the Prelude Ale. 8 Western Ave., #6, Kennebunkport, ME 04043, (207) 967-4311.

Prelude Ale

winter seasonal

(og: 1.078; abw: 6%)

Hops: Cascade, Tettnanger, Fuggles, American Goldings

Malt/grains: Pale, Crystal, Chocolate, Torrefied Wheat

Created to mark the start of the Christmas season, this nutty ale has a zesty, hoppy finish and pretty amber-glass hue.

MAINE

Sea Dog Brewing Company

 Sea Dog runs brewpubs in both Camden and Bangor, specializing in top-fermented British-style ales and the cold-fermented lagers of Central Europe. They doggedly ship beer to 21 states. 26 Front St., Bangor, ME 04401, (207) 947-8009.

Sea Dog Windjammer Blonde Ale

(og: 1.050; abw: 4.8%)

Hops: Cascade

Malts/grains: Pale, Crystal

A fresh, spirited, bubbly British-style ale with a light head, flowery bouquet, and hop flavor that lingers nicely on the tongue.

Sea Dog Old Gollywobbler Brown Ale

(og: 1.045; abw: 3.8%)

Hops: Cascade, Willamette, Tettnanger

Malts/grains: Pale, Crystal, Black Patent, Roasted Barley

Thinner than an IPA, this slightly smoky fizzy beer has a light coffee finish.

Bottled beers not photographed:

Old East India Pale Ale

(og: 1.068; abw: 6%)

Hops: Cascade, Willamette, Tettnanger

Malts/grains: Pale, Crystal, Chocolate

MAINE

Shipyard Brewing Company

A favorite of the nautical crowd (and George Bush), the Shipyard Brewery is located on Portland's industrial water-front. The brewery is built on the birth site of Henry Wadsworth Longfellow, across the street from an 1828 church that was once the heart of black community life and the site of abolitionist rallies. The facility was built in 1994 by Fred Forsley, a former real estate executive who worked with British brewery consultant Alan Pugsley. Forsley and Pugsley are now partners in an operation that includes this facility and the Kennebunkport Brewery, and are selling microbrewery packages, which include the right to brew Shipyard beers for a cost ranging from $200,000 to $1 million. In 1995, Miller Brewing Company bought 50% of the company, and plans to distribute widely on the East Coast. Shipyard's capacity was 54,000 barrels in 1995, and 108,000 barrels in 1996. 86 Newbury St., Portland, ME 04101, (800) 789-0684.

Old Thumper Extra Special Ale

(og: 1.058; abw: 5.6%)

Hops: Challenger, Progress, Goldings

Malts/grains: Pale, Crystal, Chocolate

Copper-colored with a nice head, this dryish bitter ale is made under license with the Ringwood Brewery in Hampshire, England, and won the supreme champion title at the Great British Beer Festival of 1988.

Shipyard Export Ale

(og: 1.052; abw: 5.1%)

Hops: Cascade, Willamette, Tettnanger

Malts/grains: Pale, Crystal

A dry, bitter, quaffable ale that cries out for spicy Indian food.

Blue Fin Stout

(og: 1.052; abw: 5%)

Hops: Northern Brewer, Cascade, Tettnanger, Goldings

Malts/grains: Pale, Crystal, Chocolate, Black Patent, Roasted Barley

Chamberlain Pale Ale

(og: 1.050; abw: 3.84%)

Hops: Fuggles, Cascade, Tettnanger

Malts/grains: Pale, Crystal, Chocolate

Goat Island Light Ale

(og: 1.034; abw: 2.6%)

Hops: Tettnanger, Willamette

Malts/grains: Pale, plus maize flakes

Longfellow Winter Ale

seasonal

(og: 1.062; abw: 4.8%)

Hops: Northern Brewer, Tettnanger, Cascade, Goldings

Malts/grains: Crystal, Chocolate, Roasted Barley

Mystic Seaport Pale Ale

(og: 1.050; abw: 3.84%)

Hops: Fuggles, Cascade, Tettnanger

Malts/grains: Pale, Crystal, Chocolate

MAINE

MARYLAND

Wild Goose Brewing Company

One of the first small Mid-Atlantic breweries, *Wild Goose Brewing* has been producing beer since 1989. The company is now the largest microbrewery in Maryland, producing up to 20,000 barrels of English-style ale per year. 20 Washington St., Cambridge, MD 21613, (410) 221-1121.

Snow Goose Winter Ale

winter seasonal

(og: 1.014; abw: 6.4%)

Hops: Cascade, Willamette, Fuggles, Goldings

Malts/grains: Crystal, Pale, Roasted Barley

This popular traditional English ale is coveted by beer lovers for its complex, roasty flavor, and huge hop finish.

Wild Goose Porter

(og: 1.054; abw: 5.2%)

Hops: Cascade, Willamette, Hallertauer, Tettnanger, Goldings

Malts/grains: Pale, Crystal, Chocolate, Black Patent

This voluptuous mahogany-colored ale begins with aromas of caramel, coffee, and chocolate, followed by the slightly burnt taste characteristics of this style. The hops are well balanced with the malts, with this delicious porter ending on a high (slightly bitter) note.

MARYLAND

Bottled beers not photographed:

Wild Goose Amber

(og: 1.051; abw: 5%)

Hops: Willamette, Hallertauer, Tettnanger, Cascade

Malts/grains: Pale, Crystal, Wheat, Chocolate

Wild Goose Golden Ale

(og: 1.044: abw: 4%)

Hops: Cascade, Hallertauer, Tettnanger, Goldings

Malts/grains: Pale, Wheat

Wild Goose India Pale Ale

(og: 1.056; abw: 5.25%)

Hops: Cascade, Goldings, Willamette, Tettnanger

Malts/grains: Pale, Crystal, Wheat

Wild Goose Spring Wheat Ale

spring seasonal

(og: 1.058; abw: 4.85%)

Hops: Cascade, Willamette, Czech Saaz

Malts/grains: Pale, Crystal

MASSACHUSETTS

Berkshire Brewing Company

Established in 1994 in western Massachusetts, this small (2,600 barrel) brewery produces great unfiltered, unpasteurized ales. Named after the rolling hills of the region, the brewery was started by Christopher Lalli and Gary Bogoff, who still self-distribute. 12 Railroad St., South Deerfield, MA 10373, (413) 665-6600.

Berkshire Ale

(og: 1.064; abw: 6.3%)

Hops: Bullion, Cascade, Fuggles

Malts/grains: Pale, Crystal, Caramel

This copper-colored traditional pale ale has a ribbon of caramel-malt flavor, which is filled in by a hearty hop aroma and flavor, and touched off by a sweet, yeasty accent.

Berkshire Steel Rail Extra Pale Ale

(og: 1.054; abw: 5.3%)

Hops: Kent Goldings, Willamette

Malts/grains: Two-row

Topped by an impressive head with staying power, this clear, pale gold ale has a resounding hoppy flavor and soft hoppy aftertaste.

Bottled beers not photographed:

Drayman's Porter

(og: 1.064; abw: 6.2%)

Hops: Northern Brewer, Fuggles

Malts/grains: Pale, Carapils, Crystal, Chocolate, Black Patent

Boston Beer Company

Ah, Mr. Adams, dear Mr. Adams. President Jim Koch may be infamous for his shaky claims, but he has his place in the annals of the microbrewery renaissance. Established in 1985, the Boston Beer Company brewed its first beer in Pittsburgh and, to this day, almost entirely contract-brews its beers in places other than Boston. (His Boston brewery is just a showpiece, producing only about 1%.) Harvard-educated, Koch is a fifth-generation brewer who taught mountaineering for Outward Bound before becoming a managerial consultant. He raised $400,000 to start the Boston Beer Company and, by 1996, was producing 1 million barrels per year. The first American beer exported to Germany, Sam Adams has even been spotted at presidential events and, to many Americans, is emblematic of a microbrew. Named after the rabble-rousing patriot, governor of Massachusetts, and brewer (Adams inherited a brewery on State Street from his father), the brewery is now the 14th largest in the U.S., selling over 6 million cases annually. 30 Germania St., Boston, MA 02130, (617) 522-3400.

MASSACHUSETTS

Samuel Adams Octoberfest

fall seasonal

(og: 1.056; abw: 6.3%)

Hops: Saaz, Tettnanger, Hallertauer

Malts/grains: Two-row Harrington, Caramel 60L, Munich

The color of mahogany, this dark, even-keeled lager leaves a soft malty feeling on the side of your tongue.

Samuel Adams Boston Lager

(og: 1.052; abw: 4.9%)

Hops: Hallertauer, Mittelfrueh, Tettnanger

Malts/grains: Two-row Harrington, Caramel 60L

All-malt brewing and Bavarian hops result in a sturdy lager with a lovely golden color, decent malt body, and mild spicy hop character—not as complex as the brewery advertises, but a good craft beer.

Bottled beers not photographed:

Boston Lightship

(og: 1.032; abw: 2.24%)

Hops: Saaz, Hallertauer, Mittlefrueh, Tettnanger

Malts/grains: Two-row Harrington, Caramel 60L

Samuel Adams Boston Ale

(og: 1.053; abw: 4%)

Hops: Saaz, Fuggles, Goldings

Malts/grains: Two-row Harrington, Caramel 60L

Samuel Adams Cherry Wheat

summer seasonal

(og: 1.051; abw: 4%)

Hops: Saaz, Tettnanger

Malts/grains: Two-row Harrington, Malted Wheat, Caramel 60L, Munich Wheat, plus honey and cherries

MASSACHUSETTS

Samuel Adams Cranberry Lambic

fall seasonal

(og: 1.040; abw: 3.4%)

Hops: Saaz, Tettnanger

Malts/grains: Two-row Harrington, Wheat, plus cranberries and maple syrup

Samuel Adams Cream Stout

(og: 1.056; abw: 3.4%)

Hops: Fuggles, Goldings

Malts/grains: Two-row Harrington, Malted Wheat, Roasted Unmalted Barley, Caramel 60L, Chocolate

Samuel Adams Dark Wheat

spring seasonal

(og: 1.046; abw: 3.6%)

Hops: Saaz, Tettnanger

Malts/grains: Two-row Harrington, Caramel 60L

Samuel Adams Double Bock

spring seasonal

(og: 1.084; abw: 5.76%)

Hops: Saaz, Tettnanger

Malts/grains: Two-row Harrington, Caramel 60L

Samuel Adams Honey Porter

(og: 1.059; abw: 4.7%)

Hops: Saaz, Fuggles, Goldings

Malts/grains: Two-row Harrington, Caramel 60L, Chocolate

Samuel Adams Scotch Ale

(og: 1.065; abw: 4.7%)

Hops: Fuggles, Goldings

Malts/grains: Two-row Harrington, Caramel 60L, Chocolate, Peat

Samuel Adams Triple Bock

(og: 1.717; abw: 14%)

Hops: Tettnanger, Hallertauer

Malts/grains: Two-row Harrington, Chocolate

MASSACHUSETTS

Samuel Adams Winter Lager

seasonal

(og: 1.064; abw: 4.8%)

Hops: Saaz, Kent Goldings, Tettnanger

Malts/grains: Two-row Harrington, Caramel 60L, Wheat

Massachusetts Bay Brewing

Started in 1987 with $400,000 by three guys from Harvard, Massachusetts Bay Brewing was one of the earliest microbreweries in New England (along with Catamount and D. L. Geary). They started selling Harpoon beer at two bars in Boston, and now service 3,000 restaurants and bars, with beer distributed throughout New England and down the eastern seaboard. In 1994 they produced 25,000 barrels and had some beer contract-brewed by F. X. Matt in Utica. 306 Northern Ave., Boston, MA 02210, (617) 951-4099.

Harpoon Ale

(og: 1.044; abw: 2.96%)

Hops: Cascade, Clusters

Malts/grains: Pale, Two-row, Crystal 40L

A decent enough, somewhat dry ale with a fruity accent and crisp finish. Serve with spicy foods.

Harpoon IPA

Hops: Clusters, Fuggles, Whole Leaf Cascade

Malts/grains: Pale, Two-row, Caramel 40L, Roasted Barley

Originally a summer seasonal, this popular straw-colored ale is dry, fizzy to the taste, and highly hopped.

Bottled beers not photographed:

Harpoon Golden Lager

Hops: Clusters

Malts/grains: Pale, Two-row

Harpoon Light

Hops: Clusters, Cascade

Malts/grains: Pale, Two-row

Harpoon Octoberfest

fall seasonal

Hops: Clusters

Malts/grains: Pale, Two-row, Crystal 80L

Harpoon Stout

spring seasonal

Hops: Clusters, Fuggles, Kent Goldings

Malts/grains: Pale, Two-row, Caramel 80L, Black Patent, Chocolate, Wheat

Harpoon Winter Warmer

winter seasonal

Hops: Clusters

Malts/grains: Pale, Two-row, Caramel 80L

Middlesex Brewing Company

Homebrewer Brian Friguliette started brewing in 1992, and for three years was producing approximately 300 barrels a year. He recently built a 25-barrel brewhouse, which has enabled him to increase production to 6,000 barrels a year. His beers are available only in Massachusetts at the time of this writing. 844 Woburn St., Wilmington, MA 01887, (508) 657-8100.

MASSACHUSETTS

Middlesex Brown Ale

(og: 1.044; abw: 4.2%)

Hops: Willamette, Chinook, Cascade

Malts/grains: Pale, Crystal, Munich, Chocolate

Designed as an English brown ale (made with American hops), this restrained, low-carbonated ale is good with spicy foods.

Bottled beers not photographed:

Middlesex Raspberry Wheat

(og: 1.042; abw: 4%)

Hops: Cascade

Malts/grains: Pale, Wheat

Middlesex Oatmeal Stout

(og: 1.050; abw: 4.5%)

Hops: Willamette, Chinook, Cascade

Malts/grains: Pale, Crystal, Chocolate, Roasted Barley, Oats

Mill City Brewing Company

One of the largest mill cities in New England, Lowell had many boarding houses for the workers, including one on Cabot Street, dating back to 1831 and now the home of the Mill City Brewing Company. Celebrating the city's mill heritage, the brewery features on its labels a photo of the old Harvard Brewery in Lowell (which was built it 1898 and employed 2,000 employees until it burned down in 1956). The beers are unpasteurized, with no preservatives. 199 Cabot St., Lowell, MA 01854, (508) 937-1200.

Mill City Oatmeal Stout

(og: 1.064; abw: 4.4%)

Hops: Northern Brewer, Kent Goldings

Malts/grains: Two-row Pale, Six-row Pale, Chocolate, Caramel, Roasted Barley, Oatmeal, Flaked Barley, Black Patent, Carapils, Wheat

With a creamy, modest head, this roasty stout smells and tastes of coffee, with a suggestion of chocolate.

Bottled beers not photographed:

Boarding House Ale

(og: 1.050; abw: 5.1%)

Hops: Willamette, Cascade

Malts/grains: Two-row Pale, Caramel

Chocolate Raspberry Wheat

spring seasonal

(og: 1.046; abw: 4.3%)

Hops: Northern Brewer, Cascade, Willamette

Malts/grains: Chocolate, Black Patent

Harvest Wheat

summer seasonal

(og: 1.043; abw: 3.4%)

Hops: Cascade, Mt. Hood, Tettnanger, Perle

Malts/grains: Two-row Pale, Wheat

IPA

(og: 1.055; abw: 5.9%)

Hops: Cascade, Willamette

Malts/grains: Two-row, Victory, Caramel

MASSACHUSETTS

Octoberfest

fall seasonal

(abw: 4.9%)

Hops: Saaz

Malts/grains: Munich, Vienna, Pale

Old Nutcracker

winter seasonal

(og: 1.057; abw: 5.1%)

Hops: Cascade, Willamette

Malts/grains: Two-row Pale, Caramel, Black Patent, Victory

Spindle Porter

(og: 1.051; abw: 4.8%)

Hops: Willamette, Northern Brewer, Chinook, Cascade

Malts/grains: Two-row Pale, Caramel, Black Patent, Chocolate

Old Harbor Brewing Company

This tiny brewery delivers its unfiltered, nonpasteurized beers within 72 hours of packaging. The beers are all naturally carbonated, which produces a creamy head and good mouthfeel. The company was started by homebrewers Lou Amorati, a former CPA, and John Munro, a product development manager for DuPont Chemical, who after helping a friend out at the Ipswich Brewing Company in the early 1990s decided to open a brewery. The first batch was brewed in 1995, and they are currently brewing 5,000 barrels a year. Their growlers (half-gallon jugs) are particularly popular at liquor stores throughout the state—offering fresh beer at a price that competes with the big guys' six packs. 577 Main St., Hudson, MA 01749, (508) 562-6992.

MASSACHUSETTS

Pilgrim Harvest IPA

fall seasonal

(og: 1.054; abw: 3.7%)

Hops: Northern Brewer, Nugget, Cascade, Willamette

Malts/grains: Two-row Pale, Special Roast, Crystal

Made with New England hops, this crisp, fresh beer is available after the hop harvest, which means you'll find it on the shelves in October and November.

Pilgrim Nut Brown Ale

(og: 1.048; abw: 3.5%)

Hops: Northern Brewer, Cascade

Malts/grains: Two-row Pale, Crystal, Chocolate

A strong, hoppy ale, with a burnt-caramel undertone and a long-lasting thick head.

Pilgrim Stout

winter seasonal

(og: 1.060; abw: 4%)

Hops: Northern Brewer

Malts/grains: Two-row Pale, Black Barley, Flaked Barley

A hybrid of two stout styles, this opaque stout is dry, sweet, and smoky.

Bottled beers not photographed:

Pilgrim ESB

(og: 1.052; abw: 3.6%)

Hops: Northern Brewer, Nugget, Willamette

Malts/grains: Two-row Pale, British Two-row Pale, Crystal, Chocolate

Dog's Breath Bitter

(og: 1.055; abw: 3.7%)

Hops: Nugget, Northern Brewer, Tettnanger, Cascade

Malts/grains: Two-row Pale, Crystal, Chocolate

Ould Newbury Brewing Company

Ould Newbury began in the basement of Joe and Pam Rolfe's home in the fall of 1992. They brewed 25 barrels that first year and the next year's expansion consisted of encroaching on the garage and living room, which elevated production to 125 barrels. In 1994 they moved to a 5,000-square-foot brewery in the marshy coastal town of Newburyport, and are brewing 500 barrels per year. They have a 5-barrel brewing capacity, which means they brew 155 gallons of beer at a time. They still cap by hand (note that the batch number is stamped on each cap) and all beers are bottle conditioned. 50 Park St., Newburyport, MA 01951, (508) 462-1980.

Ould Newbury Spiced Ale

winter seasonal

(og: 1.060)

Hops: Nugget, Cascade, Mt. Hood

Malts/grains: Canadian Two-row Pale, Crystal 60, plus glucose, spices

A smooth bottle-conditioned amber ale, with cinnamon, nutmeg, ginger, cloves, and a pinch of coriander thrown into the kettle.

Bottled beers not photographed:

Great Glen Scottish Ale

(og: 1.044)

Hops: Nugget, Willamette

Malts/grains: Canadian Two-row Pale, Crystal 120L, Wheat, Roasted Barley

MASSACHUSETTS

Haystack India Pale

(og: 1.055)

Hops: Nugget, Cascade

Malts/grains: Canadian Two-row Pale, Crystal 60L

Ould Newbury Porter

(og: 1.047)

Hops: Nugget, Perle, Cascade

Malts/grains: Canadian Two-row Pale, Crystal 60L, Chocolate, Black Patent, Roasted Barley

Plum Island Extra Pale

(og: 1.038)

Hops: Nugget, Tettnanger

Malts/grains: Canadian Two-row Pale, Carastan, Malted Wheat

Rye Ale

(og: 1.050)

Hops: Nugget, Perle

Malts/grains: Canadian Two-role Pale, Crystal 60L, Chocolate, Flaked Rye

Yankee Ale

(og: 1.042)

Hops: Nugget, Cascade, Willamette, Tettnanger

Malts/grains: Canadian Two-row Pale, Munich, Crystal 60L, Carastan, Chocolate

NEW YORK

Brooklyn Brewery

An *Associated Press* journalist in Kuwait in the 1970s, Stephen Hindy befriended diplomats who, out of desperation for a drink, began homebrewing. By 1986, he and his New York neighbor Tom Potter began toying with the idea of bottling Hindy's homebrew. Another neighbor, Sophia Collier (founder of Soho Natural Soda), convinced them to buy their own trucks and sell the beer themselves. They started self-distributing and, by 1991, were also distributing Sierra Nevada, Catamount, and others who'd had a hard time breaking into the New York market. Brooklyn Brewery contract-brews at F. X. Matt in Utica, and has a brewery in a former matzo bakery to produce draft seasonals for the New York market. Interested in the borough's rich brewing heritage, Brooklyn's labels (designed by Milton Glaser) conjure up the Dodgers, Brooklyn Bridge, and the days before prohibition, when 50 breweries were in the borough. Ruminated Hindy to *Modern Brewing Age* about his life's course, "Running across the street when people are shooting guns on the street is scary, but it's kind of a thrill. You get to the other side, and it's a rush. But starting a business, you feel like people are shooting up and down the street all the time. And if they hit you, you know you're going down, and so are all your investors and people who believe in you and who you owe money to and with whom you have relationships. It's the fear of that that keeps you going." 79 N. 11th St., Brooklyn, NY 11211, (718) 486-7422.

Brooklyn Black Chocolate Stout

winter seasonal

(og: 1.084; abw: 8.2%)

Hops: Fuggles, Willamette

Malts/grains: Two-row Pale, Caramel, Chocolate, Wheat, Black Barley, Roasted Barley

This limited winter edition is black as pitch, with a creamy luscious head, rich robust body, and loads of taste in every swallow. With chocolate overtones, this glorious stout is slightly sweet, with a mellow maltiness and hoppy aftertaste.

Brooklyn Brown Ale

(og: 1.060; abw: 5.7%)

Hops: Cascade, Northern Brewer, Willamette

Malts/grains: Pale, Crystal, Chocolate, Roasted Barley, Biscuit

Fragrant with a hint of spice and chocolate, this gutsy, refreshingly bitter ale has an assertive fruity finish.

Brooklyn East India Pale Ale

summer seasonal

(og: 1.067; abw: 7%)

Hops: Kent Goldings, Cascade, Willamette

Malts/grains: Two-row English Pipkin, Halcyon Pale Ale, Two-row English Pilsner, Caramel, Wheat

With a rich creamy head and a cloudy golden red color, this well-balanced IPA offers a passing malt reference before giving in to floral undertones and a dry bitter finish.

Brooklyn Lager

(og: 1.052; abw: 5.1%)

Hops: Cascade, Hallertauer

Malts/grains: Two-row Pale Malt, Caramel, Carapils

Brewed according to a pre-prohibition recipe, this naturally carbonated lager is the color of burnt sierra, with a complex floral aroma and malty palate.

NEW YORK

F. X. Matt Brewing Company

 Founded in 1888 by immigrant Francis Xavier Matt (who had worked at the Duke of Baden Brewery in Germany), this company survived prohibition by selling soft drinks under the Utica Club trademark. Reintroducing beer under the Utica Club trademark after prohibition was repealed, F. X. Matt became one of the most successful regional breweries. Today the third generation leads the firm. While not a microbrewery (they are the 12th largest brewery in the U.S.), F. X. Matt is a good regional brewery, and the contract brewer of choice for many, including Dock Street, Brooklyn Lager, and New Amsterdam. The younger generation became interested in quality lagers after visiting the Black Forest and tasting the Bavarian beers of southern Germany and, as a result, Saranac Adirondack Lager was introduced (which won GABF awards in 1991 and 1992), followed by other specialty beers. 811 Edward St., Utica, NY 13502, (315) 732-3181.

Saranac Black & Tan

(og: 1.016; abw: 3.85%)

Hops: Cascade, German Hallertauer, English Goldings, American Hallertauer

Malts/grains: Chocolate, Black Patent, Roasted Barley, Caramel, Crystal

This melding of an Irish stout with a German lager produces a delicious, nearly opaque hybrid with a sweet malty flavor, bitter roasty finish, and lingering lacy head.

Saranac Pale Ale

(og: 1.055; abw: 4.3%)

Hops: Kent Goldings, Cascade

Malts/grains: British Pale

F. X. Matt added this aggressively hopped pale ale to their line of lagers, which has a great fruity hop bouquet reminiscent of apricots. With a pleasant soft taste, this dark amber-colored ale is a good example of the pale ale style, and won the Best Pale Ale award at the 1994 U.S. Beer Festival.

NEW YORK

Bottled beers not photographed:

Saranac Adirondack Amber

(og: 1.010; abw: 4%)

Hops: Hallertauer, Mt. Hood, Clusters, Cascade

Malts/grains: Two-row, Caramel

Note: Formerly called Saranac Adirondack Lager, this is the repackaged Saranac 1888 from a decade ago.

Saranac Chocolate Amber

spring seasonal

(og: 1.058; abw: 4.4%)

Hops: German Northern Brewer, Hallertauer Hersbrucker, two undisclosed U.S. varieties

Malts/grains: Munich, Chocolate, Two-row, Wheat, Caramel

Saranac Golden Pilsner

(og: 1.010; abw: 3.9%)

Hops: Cascade, Clusters, Tettnanger

Malts/grains: Barley, Wheat

Saranac Mountain Berry Ale

summer seasonal

Hops: Clusters, Cascade

Malts/grains: Chocolate, Wheat, Caramel

Saranac Season's Best

winter seasonal

Hops: Clusters, Cascade

Malts/grains: Chocolate, Belgian

Saranac Wild Berry Wheat

(abw: 4.1%)

Hops: Saaz, Perle

Malts/grains: Wheat, Caramel

NEW YORK

New Amsterdam Company

Founded in 1982, the New Amsterdam Company is named after the Dutch settlement of 1624 that later became Manhattan. F. X. Matt bought the brand in the 1980s, then sold it in 1990 to Chatham Imports, a beverage supply company owned by Joe Magliocco, a Yale-trained lawyer with a penchant for fine wines and art history. The son of a wine importer, Magliocco considers New Amsterdam the "Chateau Mouton Rothschild of beer," and has emulated that winery by featuring artwork each year by a well-known artist on his Winter anniversary label. In the past few years he's commissioned labels by Jennifer Bartlett and Ross Bleckner, and donates a portion of the proceeds to charity. Beautiful to look at, the beers are also pretty tasty, and have garnered a number of people's choice awards at the Great American Beer Festival. The beer is brewed in Utica. Corporate office: 257 Park Ave. S., 7th floor, New York, NY 10010, (212) 473-1100.

New Amsterdam Amber

(og: 1.031; abw: 3.2%)

Hops: Cascade, Hallertauer

Malts/grains: Two-row Roasted Barley

New Amsterdam's flagship beer, this complex, herbal amber has a luscious floral bouquet and creamy flavor. Delicious with hearty foods.

New Amsterdam New York Ale

(og: 1.048; abw: 5%)

Hops: Hallertauer, Cascade

Malts/grains: Two-row Roasted Barley, Caramel

An aromatic dry-hopped beer that stands up to spicy foods.

NEW YORK

New Amsterdam Winter Anniversary New York Dark Ale 1995

In celebration of the founding of the city of New Amsterdam in 1624, this limited 1995 winter release features a label with a painting by Ross Bleckner. The color of dark chocolate, this full-headed ale has a strong malty character, with hints of roasted toffee and winter spices. A good dessert beer.

Bottled beers not photographed:

New Amsterdam Black & Tan

(og: 1.050; abw: 5%)

Hops: Clusters, Fuggles, Kent Goldings, Hallertauer, Cascade

Malts/grains: Two-row Roasted Barley, Caramel, Wheat, Chocolate, Black Patent, Flaked Oats, Roasted Barley

New Amsterdam Blonde Lager

(og: 1.046; abw: 4.95%)

Hops: Tettnanger, Czech Saaz, Cascade

Malts/grains: Two-row Roasted Barley, Belgian Caravienne, Belgian Wheat

New Amsterdam India Dark Ale

(og: 1.049; abw: 5%)

Hops: Northern Brewer, Clusters

Malts/grains: Victory, Two-row Roasted Barley, Caramel, Roasted Barley, Chocolate, Black Patent

Old World Brewing Company

Sal Pennachio began homebrewing 15 years ago, working on Wall Street during the day and toiling in his basement on Staten Island at night. He began bottling in 1992, creating a beer that, in the words of The New York Times, is "too rich to swill by the six-pack and too noble to spend life as a chaser for nachos and ballpark franks." The beer is brewed at Stevens Point Brewery in Wisconsin. Corporate office: 2070 Victory Blvd., Staten Island, NY 10314, (718) 370-0551.

New York Style Harbor Dark Ale

(og: 1.056; abw: 4.32%)

Hops: Willamette, Cascade

Malts/grains: Pale, Caramel, Chocolate, Black Patent

This light-tasting porter has a hint of chocolate, with a subtle hoppiness that's not overpowering.

New York Style Harbor Amber Ale

(og: 1.052; 4.1%)

Hops: Chinook, Cascade, Hallertauer

Malts/grains: Pale, Two-row, Munich, Caramel

With a fruity aroma, this simple, clear ale is easy drinking, with a slight hop finish. Closer to an ESB than a pale ale.

NEW YORK

Spring Street Brewing Company

Spring Street was founded in 1993 by Andrew Klein, a Harvard-trained Manhattan attorney who wanted to make great Belgian beer. In the 1400s, before the wide use of hops, Belgian brewers used other ingredients to soften the bitter sourness of beer, which was made primarily with wheat (hence the name, "witbier"). Spanish oranges brought home by Flemish traders or spices from the East Indies were commonly used. By the 1800s, with the ascendance of hop-based beers in England and Germany, Belgian brewers turned to hop spicing and barley-based beers, and the popularity of witbier diminished. The style was resurrected in the 1960s, and today there are more than 40 brands of witbier. Klein's beer is brewed in Minnesota by Herm Hegger, who for 15 years was a leading brewer of Belgian ales at Brouwerij Raaf in Holland. Corporate office: 60 Spring St., New York, NY 10012, (800) 948-8988.

Wit Amber Harvest 1444 Recipe

(og: 1.050; abw: 5.3%)

Hops: Tettnanger, Clusters

Malts/grains: Wheat, Roasted Wheat, Barley, Roasted Barley

With a lathery full head and a true amber color, this dark wheat is fuller bodied than the original (see below). Velvety smooth and remarkably mild, it begs to be swallowed, with a flowery bouquet and a slight caramel taste laced with a hint of whiskey.

Wit Original 1444 Recipe

(og: 1.046; abw: 4.8%)

Hops: Tettnanger, Clusters

Malts/grains: Wheat, Barley

Spanish orange peel and coriander are added in the initial boil of this unfiltered white ale that is historically associated with the eastern provinces of Belgium. Brewed from wheat, it has a cloudy wheat color, with a light, tangy wheat taste that is almost cidery, and finishes very quickly. A good summer beer.

Woodstock Brewing Company

In the beautiful Hudson Valley (known for its wealth of breweries before prohibition), this brewery was built in a former foundry that dates back to the early 1800s. Unpasteurized, the beer is brewed with Catskill Mountain water. 20 St. James Ct., Kingston, NY 12401-1000, (914) 331-2810.

Big Indian Porter

(og: 1.070; abw: 5.7%)

Hops: Clusters, Hallertauer, Tettnanger

Malts/grains: Two-row, Crystal, Chocolate, Black Patent

This is a big, rich porter—almost a stout—packed with a nice chocolate malt and roasted barley flavor.

St. James Ale

(og: 1.042; abw: 3.6%)

Hops: Clusters, Cascade

Malts/grains: Two-row, Vienna, Caramel

This crisp, clean ale has a flowery aroma, a thick creamy head, and a rich golden color.

Bottled beers not photographed:

Hudson Lager

(og: 1.051: abw: 4.2%)

Hops: Hallertauer, Tettnanger

Malts/grains: Two-row, Munich

NEW YORK

Ichabod Crane Holiday Lager

winter seasonal

(og: 1.098; abw: 8.6%)

Hops: Clusters, Hallertauer

Malts/grains: Two-row, Munich, Caramel, plus nutmeg, cinnamon stick, cloves, pumpkin

PENNSYLVANIA

Arrowhead Brewing Company

Francis Mead is a former assistant director of clinical trials at Smith-Kline Pharmaceuticals who read Charlie Papazian's Complete Joy of Homebrewing and started brewing. At UC Davis, he met Dave Geary (of the D. L. Geary Brewing Company in Maine) and became his apprentice. There he hooked up with Alan Pugsley, an English brewer with a degree in brewing biochemistry, who set him up with an all-grain simple infusion system typical of an English ale brewhouse. Mead brewed his first batch of ale using a top-fermenting yeast and open fermentation process in 1991, and currently has the capacity for 6,000 barrels. Arrowhead is located at the site of a battleground in the French and Indian War, a nod to the history of Chambersburg. Arrowhead is currently weathering bankruptcy, and beer lovers are hoping the company will make it. 1667 Orchard Dr., Chambersburg, PA 17201, (717) 264-0101.

Red Feather Pale Ale

(og: 1.047; abw: 4.7%)

Hops: Cascade, Northern Brewer, Willamette

Malts/grains: English Two-row

With a rich creamy lingering head, this chestnut-colored ale has a medium body, and mild fruity bouquet suggestive of bananas and vanilla. Not bitter like a pale ale can be, this delicious beer balances the hop and malt well, and concludes with a light hop finish.

Brewery Hill Brewing Company

Decades ago in Pennsylvania, there were breweries in most towns. There was a big brewery on the hill in Wilkes-Barre, and this modern-day brewery was named in a nod to that heritage. Doing business also as the Lion Brewery, Brewery Hill was started in 1993 by Leo Orlandini when he introduced his black and tan. 700 N. Pennsylvania Ave., Wilkes-Barre, PA 18703, (717) 823-8801.

Brewery Hill Honey Amber

(og: 1.051; abw: 5.5%)

Hops: Kent Goldings, Saaz, Mt. Hood, Hallertauer Hersbrucker

Malts/grains: Pale, Two-row, Caramel 60L, plus honey

A smooth, well balanced beer with a distinct touch of honey, won a bronze medal at World Beer Cup in 1996.

Bottled beers not photographed:

Brewery Hill Black & Tan

(og: 1.052; abw: 5.2%)

Hops: Kent Goldings, Tettnanger, Mt. Hood, Saaz, Hallertauer Hersbrucker

Malts/grains: Two-row Pale, Caramel 60L, Chocolate

Brewery Hill Cherry Wheat

spring seasonal

(og: 1.052; abw: 5%)

Hops: Northern Brewer, Cascade

Malts/grains: Two-row Pale, Wheat, Caramel 60L

Brewery Hill Pale Ale

(og: 1.052; abw: 5.2%)

Hops: Cascade, Mt. Hood

Malts/grains: Two-row Pale, Caramel 60L, Carapils

PENNSYLVANIA

Dock Street Brewing Company

Inspired by the British "Campaign for Real Ale" in the 1970s (a reaction to British brewing conglomerates and the disappearance of cask-conditioned ales in the pubs), sculptor Jeff Ware opened the Dock Street Brewery & Restaurant in Philadelphia (next to the Four Seasons Hotel) and, more recently, one in Washington D.C. in the historic Warner Theater building. His beers are contract-brewed in Utica. Corporate office: 225 City Line Ave., Suite 110, Bala Cynwyd, PA 19004, (610) 668-1480. (Dock Street Brewery and Restaurant is located at Two Logan Square, Philadelphia, PA 19103, (215) 496-0413.

Dock Street Bohemian USA

(og: 1.050; abw: 4.27%)

Hops: Czech Saaz, Hallertauer

Malts/grains: Two-row Barley, Munich, Carapils

This classic Bohemian pilsner is characterized by its golden color and soft complex malty flavor. With a gentle hop bitterness, it is light-bodied, with a long dry finish.

Dock Street Illuminator USA

(og: 1.072; abw: 6%)

Hops: Tettnanger, Hallertauer

Malts/grains: Two-row Barley, Caramel, Munich, Carapils

A seasonal slightly cloudy double-bock with a big malt flavor and thick lacy cappuccino head. Some feel it's not heavy or complex enough to claim the "ator" suffix.

Bottled beers not photographed:

Dock Street Amber Beer

(og: 1.050; abw: 4.28%)

Hops: Cascade

Malts/grains: Two-row, Caramel

PENNNSYLVANIA

Jones Brewing Company

In 1907, William B. "Stoney" Jones (a Welsh immigrant and the grandfather of actress Shirley Jones) built the Eureka Brewing Company on the banks of the Youghiogheny River. The immigrants in the western part of the state who had trouble pronouncing the brewery's name asked instead for a Stoney's, and the name stuck. Today the Jones Brewing company is the 18th largest brewery in the United States, contracting beers such as Penn Pilsner. Auto parts dealer Gabby Podlucky took over the brewery in 1988 from the Jones family, though a fourth-generation Jones remained as brewmaster. Located near Pittsburgh, they produce all-grain beer with no additives, and hope to emulate their neighbor, Rolling Rock. "Rolling Rock taught us one thing for sure: be prepared, because it might happen to you!" They're hoping. 254 Second St., Smithton, PA 15479, (412) 872-6626.

Eureka 1881 Red Irish Amber Lager

(og: 1.009; abw: 3.5%)

Hops: Clusters

Malts/grains: Barley, plus corn grits

A mild Irish amber brewed with a semi-sweet caramel malt.

Eureka Black & Tan Welsh Dark

(og: 1.012; abw: 3.5%)

Hops: Clusters

Malts/grains: Caramel, plus corn grits

Half lager, half porter, this clear dark beer is not particularly strong, with a light hoppy taste and no aftertaste.

Stoney's Beer

(og: 1.042; abw: 3.55%)

Hops: Clusters

Malts/grains: Barley, plus corn grits

Brewed for nearly 90 years, Stoney's is an easy lager with an unobtrusive flavor, typical of a mainstream American lager.

Stoney's Light Beer

(og: 1.019; abw: 3.2%)

Hops: Clusters

Malts/grains: Barley, plus corn grits

With a short-lasting head, this clear, golden beer is very light, with minimal flavor and an almost watery taste.

Bottled beers not photographed:

Esquire Extra Dry

(og: 1.044; abw: 3.85%)

Hops: Clusters

Malts/grains: Barley, plus corn grits

Eureka Gold Lager

(og: 1.009; abw: 3.54%)

Hops: Clusters

Malts/grains: Barley, plus corn grits

Eureka Gold Light Lager

(og: 1.005; abw: 3.09%)

Hops: Clusters

Malts/grains: Barley, plus corn grits

Pennsylvania Brewing Company

Tom Pastorius' family founded one of the first German settlements in America, in Germantown, Pennsylvania in 1683, and he is trying to carry on the tradition, running the first Tied House (brewery-owned restaurant) in Pennsylvania since prohibition. Located in the historic Eberhardt & Ober Brewery building in the German section of Pittsburgh, his brewpub serves German lagers and food that will make you think you are in Bavaria, including kasseler rippchen (pork chops), wiener schnitzel, and sauerbraten. Pastorius established the company in 1986 and introduced his flagship brand, Penn Pilsner, at the City Tavern in Philadelphia. (The Tied House opened in 1989.) One of the earliest microbreweries in the eastern United States (and the first in the state), Pennsylvania Brewing produces 10,000 barrels yearly, and was selected as one of the top 24 American beers by Michael Jackson in 1995. Troy Hill Rd. & Vinial St., Pittsburgh, PA 15212. Office: (412) 237-9400. Restaurant: (412) 237-9402.

Helles Gold

(og: 1.046: abw: 3.6%)

Hops: Hallertauer

Malts/grains: Two-row Barley, Special Roasted Barley

Each year, the folks at Hallertau (a town in Bavaria) celebrate the hop harvest with a hop queen, and drink a beer quite similar to Helles Gold. With a medium lasting head and clear golden color, this is a mild, clean-tasting, outdoorsy lager.

Penn Dark

(og: 1.051; abw: 4%)

Hops: Hallertauer

Malts/grains: Two-row Barley, Special Roasted Barley

A smooth, full bodied beer in the style of a Muenchner Dunkelstyle lager, with a well balanced bitterness and hop aroma. The label features the Valkyries who, according to Norse legend, sent slain warriors to Valhalla for eternal feasting and drinking.

Penn Pilsner

(og: 1.050; abw: 4%)

Hops: Hallertauer

Malts/grains: Two-row Barley, Special Roasted Barley

The malts lend this delicious beer a slightly dark roast taste that's unusual for a pilsner. With a faded copper color, this is a smooth bright beer that goes down easy and fast.

Stoudt Brewing Company

This Lancaster County microbrewery (located in the hamlet of *Adamstown*—population 1,000) was started in 1987 by Carol Stoudt, who while honeymooning in Germany twenty years ago got the notion with her husband to make German-style lagers. The mother of five, Carol Stoudt is arguably the first woman to head a microbrewery in the United States, and has a tremendous following among beer lovers. Proclaimed "the best in Pennsylvania" by Michael Jackson, Stoudt's has racked up an impressive number of Great American Beer Festival medals, and claims the partial secret of its success is the pure water from the Susquehanna Aquifer. Route 272, Adamstown, PA 19501, (717) 484-4655.

Stoudt's Gold

(og: 1.052; abw: 4.5%)

Hops: Clusters, Hallertauer

Malts/grains: Two-row, Munich, Crystal

A favorite of beer lovers, Stoudt's signature beer is smooth and full bodied, with a malt emphasis.

Stoudt's Honey Double Mai Bock

spring seasonal

(og: 1.068; abw: 6%)

Hops: Perle, Clusters, Hallertauer, Saaz

Malts/grains: Two-row, Munich, Crystal

Carol Stoudt took a golden double bock and added more malts, less water, and a touch of honey. This soft, malty, straw-colored beer has a nice depth, distinctive hop bitterness, and beautifully rounded mouthfeel. The honey taste is soft and subtle.

Bottled beers not photographed:

Fat Dog Stout

(og: 1.064; abw: 5%)

Hops: Fuggles, Goldings

Malts/grains: Two-row, Munich, Chocolate, Black Patent, Victory, Crystal

Stoudt's Abbey Double

(og: 1.072; abw: 6%)

Hops: Perle, Tettnanger, Clusters, Hallertauer

Malts/grains: Two-row, Munich, Crystal

Stoudt's Abbey Triple

(og: 1.080; abw: 7%)

Hops: Perle, Tettnanger, Clusters, Hallertauer

Malts/grains: Two-row, Munich, Crystal

Stoudt's Ale

(og: 1.052; abw: 4.5%)

Hops: Willamette

Malts/grains: Two-row, Crystal

Stoudt's Amber

(og: 1.056; abw: 5%)

Hops: Cascade

Malts/grains: Two-row, Munich, Crystal

Stoudt's Bock

(og: 1.064; abw: 6%)

Hops: Hallertauer, Perle, Tettnanger, Clusters

Malts/grains: Two-row, Munich, Crystal

Stoudt's Fest

(og: 1.052; abw: 4%)

Hops: Clusters, Hallertauer, Tettnanger

Malts/grains: Two-row, Munich, Crystal

Stoudt's Honey Double Bock

(og: 1.072%; abw: 6.5%)

Hops: Perle, Tettnanger, Clusters, Hallertauer.

Malts/grains: Two-row, Munich, Crystal

Stoudt's Pilsner

(og: 1.050; abw: 4%)

Hops: Perle, Clusters, Saaz

Malts/grains: Two-row, Wheat

Tun Tavern Brewing Company

English-born Samuel Carpenter moved to Philadelphia in 1683. There, he made a deal with William Penn to build the city's longest wharf— one that could hold a whopping 12 ships—on a strip of land that held an artesian well. This well was renowned to be the best in the city so, in 1685, Carpenter decided to build Tun Tavern (tun being a measur-ing term for casks of beer). The masons held their first meeting there in 1732, Peggy Mullen dished up the first Philadelphia cheese steak at the tavern ten years later and, in 1775, the Second Continental Con-gress established the marines here and made it their headquarters. The tavern burned in 1782, and now a freeway covers the site. But in 1989 the marines reconstructed the tavern downtown on the corner of Front and Spruce Streets, and former marine Monty Dahm began brewing this beer as a fundraiser for the tavern (which doesn't have its own brew-ery—the beer is brewed by Lion in Wilkes-Barre). Corporate office: 947 Old York Rd., Abington, PA 19001, (215) 887-8819.

Tun Tavern Lager

(og: 1.004; abw: 3.56%)

Hops: Saaz, Mt. Hood

Malts/grains: Caramel, Munich

This Vienna-style amber lager has a modestly hoppy flavor that pleasantly rolls along.

VERMONT

Catamount Brewing Company

Founded in 1986 by homebrewer Stephen Mason in a former meat-packing factory near Dartmouth College, this Vermont company has rapidly grown into a critically acclaimed microbrewery. The company takes its name from a breed of mountain lion that once roamed New England and is beginning to make a comeback. New York Magazine proclaimed Catamount's Christmas ale refined and robust—"A Sean Connery in an age of Pierce Brosnans." 58 S. Main St., White River Junction, VT 05001, (802) 296-2248.

Catamount Amber

(og: 1.123; abw: 4%)

Hops: Galena, Willamette

Malts/grains: Six-row, Caramel 40L, Carapils

With a pronounced hoppiness from the carbonation, this honest grainy-tasting beer has great hop-malt character. Enjoy it on a fall afternoon with a crisp apple and a hunk of Vermont cheddar.

Catamount Octoberfest

fall seasonal

(og: 1.056; abw: 4.4%)

Hops: Northern Brewer, Tettnanger

Malts/grains: Two-row, Caramel, Munich

This Vienna-style amber lager with its deep golden autumn color has a smooth malt character that is enhanced by a spicy hop accent.

Bottled beers not photographed:

Catamount American Wheat

spring/summer seasonal

(og: 1.042; abw: 3.53%)

Hops: Kent Goldings, Hallertauer

Malts/grains: Two-row, Malted Wheat

Catamount Bock

spring seasonal

(og: 1.064)

Hops: Northern Brewer, Hallertauer

Malts/grains: Two-row, Caramel 90L, Caramel 40L, Munich 10L

Catamount Christmas Ale

seasonal

(og: 1.058; abw: 4.2%)

Hops: Cascade

Malts/grains: Six-row, Caramel, Munich, Carapils, Black Patent, Wheat

Catamount Gold

(og: 1.045; abw: 3.6%)

Hops: Willamette

Malts/grains: Six-row, Carapils, Caramel 40L

VERMONT

Catamount Pale Ale

(og: 1.049)

Hops: Cascade, Kent Goldings

Malts/grains: Two-row, Caramel 40L, Carapils, Black Patent

Catamount Porter

(og: 1.053; abw: 4.2%)

Hops: Galena, Cascade

Malts/grains: Six-row, Caramel, Carapils, Black Roasted Barley, Black Barley

Long Trail Brewing Company

 In 1989, six years after the first keg of Long Trail Ale was tapped in the basement of a former woolen mill in Bridgewater, Vermont, the Mountain Brewers moved to a 15,000-square-foot facility two miles down the road and changed their name to Long Trail Brewing, in a nod to the great hiking in these parts. When they moved, they even released a Hit the Trail Ale, which has taken its place among their staple beers. At the junction of U.S. Route 4 and Vermont Route 100A, Bridgewater Corners, VT 05034, (802) 672-5011.

Long Trail Ale

(og: 1.046; abw: 5%)

Hops: Willamette, Cascade

Malts/grains: Two-row, Crystal, Chocolate

Their flagship, this sprightly, malty, well-made ale has a subtle but enduring hop bitterness.

Long Trail Hibernator

winter seasonal

(og: 1.058; abw: 5.9%)

Hops: Willamette

Malts/grains: Two-row, Crystal, Chocolate, Black Malt, plus honey

This great winter brew is a pretty chestnut color, with a creamy head and medium body. The abundant flavor starts before you actually taste it, with the piney spices coming through. It's fresh and interesting, fairly sweet (almost 1 ounce of honey per bottle), with a clean aftertaste.

Bottled beers not photographed:

Double Bag Ale

Dusseldorf-style double alt

(og: 1.065; abw: 5.76%)

Malts/grains: Two-row Pale, Crystal, Chocolate

Harvest Ale

fall seasonal

(abw: 3.4%)

Hops: Vermont Cascade

Malts/grains: Two-row Pale, Crystal

Long Trail Kolsch

(og: 1.045; abw: 4.1%)

Hops: German varieties

Malts/grains: Two-row Pale, Wheat Malt

Long Trail Stout

(og: 1.045; abw: 4.3%)

Hops: Chinook

Malts/grains: Two-row Pale, Chocolate

VERMONT

McNeill's Brewery

This brewpub was built by Ray and Holiday McNeill in a former Victorian firehouse in Brattleboro, Vermont. Spicy chili is a specialty of the house, which can be quenched with the 10 unfiltered ales on tap, plus seasonals. Their 22-ounce bottles are distributed in southern Vermont. 90 Elliot St., Brattleboro, VT 05301, (802) 254-2553.

Duck's Breath Ale

(og: 1.048; abw: 4.3%)

Hops: Kent Goldings

Malts/grains: British Maris Otter, Crystal

The dry hopping dominates in this fresh bottle-conditoned ale.

McNeill's Firehouse Amber Ale

(og: 1.048; abw: 4%)

Hops: Kent Goldings

Malts/grains: Two-row Pale, Crystal

With a robust, short-lived head, this clear medium amber-colored ale has a strong hoppy flavor and mild aftertaste.

McNeill's Oatmeal Stout

(og: 1.058; abw: 4.1%)

Hops: Fuggles

Malts/grains: Pale, Crystal, Chocolate, Black Patent, Munich, Roasted Barley, Flaked Oats, plus dextrin

This thick, rich, jet black stout is beefed up with many kinds of malts. It's malty, dark, a bit sweet, and very good.

Bottled beers not photographed:

Dead Horse IPA

(og: 1.056)

Hops: Kent Goldings

Malts/grains: Pale, Crystal, plus dextrin

Alle Tage Altbier

(og: 1.046)

Hops: German Noble

Big Nose Blond

(og: 1.046)

Hops: Northern Brewer, Cascade, Hallertauer

Malts/grains: Wheat, Munich, Crystal, Pale, Two-row

Pullman's Porter

(og: 1.054)

Hops: Northern Brewer, Cascade

Malts/grains: Pale, Chocolate, Black Patent, Roasted Barley, Crystal

McNeill's ESB

(og: 1.054)

Hops: Cascade

Malts/grains: Pale, Crystal

Champ Ale

(og: 1.050)

Hops: Cascade

Malts/grains: Pale, Crystal

VERMONT

Otter Creek Brewing

Lawrence Miller first caught the brew bug while attending Reed College in Oregon. In 1989, he bought *Widmer Brewing*'s equipment and chose the college town of Middlebury for its lifestyle and good water. Miller first shipped beer locally in 1991, resisting the urge to ship out of state until he felt ready (it would take another four years). He began bottling in 1993, and the response was so overwhelming that his recently doubled production capacity was quickly outstripped. Efforts to satisfy demand resulted in strong growth in 1994 and 1995. Construction of a new brewery with a capacity of 40,000 barrels allows Miller to sell outside of Vermont (and makes those of us in neighboring states very happy). Trivia question: can you find the otter on every label? Some Vermonter's claim that Otter Creek's seasonal beers are the only way to recognize the change in season in this snowy region. 85 Exchange St., Middlebury, VT 05753, (802) 388-0727.

Otter Creek Copper Ale

(og: 1.050; abw: 4.16%)

Hops: Chinook, Hallertauer, Tettnanger

Malts/grains: Two-row Pale, Munich, Caramel 20L and 40L, Carapils, Roasted Barley

The flagship, this slightly hazy amber ale is smooth as silk and well balanced, with a nice malty nose and strong hop finish.

Otter Creek Hickory Switch Smoked Amber Ale

fall seasonal

(og: 1.050; abw: 3.92%)

Hops: Chinook, Hallertauer, Tettnanger, Cascade, Willamette

Malts/grains: Two-row Pale, Munich, Caramel 60L, Carapils, Chocolate

Brewed with malts roasted over hickory wood at the brewery, this medium-bodied mildly-hopped ale has a subtle smokiness that is complimented by the underlying caramel and malt flavors.

VERMONT

Bottled beers not photographed:

Helles Alt Beer

(og: 1.043; abw: 3.6%)

Hops: Chinook, American Hallertauer, American Tettnanger

Malts/grains: Two-row Pale, Munich, Carapils

Mud Bock Spring Ale

spring seasonal

(og: 1.059; abw: 4.64%)

Hops: Cascade

Malts/grains: Two-row Pale, Munich, Caramel 20L and 40L, Carapils, Chocolate, Wheat

Stovepipe Porter

winter seasonal

(og: 1.054; abw: 4.4%)

Hops: Chinook, Cascade, Willamette

Malts/grains: Two-row Pale, Munich, Caramel 60L, Chocolate, Carapils, Roasted Barley

Summer Wheat Ale

summer seasonal

(og: 1.038; abw: 3.28%)

Hops: Willamette, Cascade

Malts/grains: Two-row Pale, Wheat

VERMONT

RECIPES

Cooking tips:

 When cooking with beer, bring the beer to room temperature for the best flavor.

 The average 12-ounce bottle measures $1^1/_2$ cups.

The longer the cooking process, the more subtle the beer taste seems to be. For a sharper, more pronounced beer flavor, reserve 2 to 3 tablespoons to add near the end of cooking.

Tomato Herb Soup with Chipotle Cream

SERVES 6 TO 8 GENEROUSLY

Beer mellows the acidity of tomatoes and enriches this vegetarian soup, making it a welcoming lunch with French bread for the slopes, picnics, or poolside. Serve hot or cold, changing herbs with the season.

    3 tablespoons olive oil
    1 large onion, diced
    2 large stalks celery with leaves, diced
    2 large carrots, peeled and diced
    3 large cloves garlic, chopped
    2 tablespoons tomato paste
    2 (28-ounce) cans plum tomatoes
    5 cups vegetable stock
    1 cup amber beer such as Anderson Valley Boont Amber
    1/2 cup chopped fresh basil plus 1/2 cup chiffonade of
        fresh basil for garnish
    1/4 cup chopped fresh flat-leaf parsley
    2 tablespoons fresh thyme leaves
    1/4 teaspoon ground allspice
    1 teaspoon salt
    1 teaspoon ground black pepper

Chipotle Cream:

    1 canned chipotle in adobo
    1 cup sour cream or crème fraîche
    1/2 teaspoon salt
    3 tablespoons light cream

In a large stockpot, heat oil over medium heat. Add onion, celery, carrot, and garlic. Stir to coat, cover, and sweat vegetables until they begin to soften, stirring occasionally, 5 to 8 minutes. Add the tomato paste and stir to distribute thoroughly.

Add tomatoes, stock, beer, chopped basil, and remaining herbs, spices, salt, and pepper. Cover and bring to a boil. Uncover and simmer over medium heat, stirring often to break up tomatoes, 45 minutes.

Put the soup solids into a food processor in 2 or 3 batches, and pulse a few times to break up the tomato chunks and other vegetables (do not purée). Return liquid to pot. Gently heat the soup a few more minutes.

Meanwhile, make the chipotle cream. Combine all ingredients in a blender until smooth. Place in a small bowl and set aside for garnish.

To serve, ladle the soup into bowls. Top with a dollop of the chipotle cream and garnish with basil chiffonade.

NOTE: Some flavors are subdued when served cold. If serving this soup cold, to enhance the beer flavor, stir in an additional 1/4 cup beer just before serving.

Corn and Scallop Chowder

SERVES **8**

As a child, I'd go scalloping on Buzzard's Bay with my parents, taking the pearly shellfish hom to panfry them. If your catch is small, serving it in soup makes a little go a long way. Searing the scallops before adding to the chowder keeps them tender.

6 ears corn, husked, or 3 cups kernels

$1/4$ pound bacon, diced small, for garnish

2 tablespoons unsalted butter

3 leeks, trimmed well and diced

1 yellow onion, diced small

2 medium stalks celery with leaves, diced

$1^1/2$ pounds red potatoes (unpeeled), diced

4 sprigs fresh thyme

$3/4$ cup amber beer such as Wild Boar Special Amber

6 cups fish stock

$1/4$ teaspoon cayenne powder

Freshly ground black pepper to taste

$1^1/2$ pounds sea scallops

1 to 2 tablespoons olive oil

Salt and pepper

1 cup whole milk

Chopped fresh parsley, for garnish

Place the corn in a large stockpot of boiling water and cook until tender, 3 to 5 minutes. Drain, and reserve 1 cup of the cooking liquid. When corn is cool enough to handle, remove the kernels with a sharp knife and set aside.

In the same stockpot, wiped dry, cook the bacon over medium heat 8 to 10 minutes or until crisp. Set aside on paper towel. Add the butter to the bacon fat and stir to melt. Add the leeks, onion, and celery. Sauté over medium heat, uncovered, until soft and translucent but not brown, 3 to 5 minutes. Add potatoes and stir to coat with butter and oil.

Add thyme, beer, fish stock, 1 cup reserved corn liquid, cayenne powder, and black pepper. Cover, bring to a boil, reduce heat to medium, and simmer, partially covered, until potatoes are tender, 20 to 25 minutes.

Meanwhile, heat grill, broiler, or a sauté pan to medium-high. Pat dry the scallops, then brush with olive oil and season with salt and pepper. Sear scallops 3 to 4 minutes per side. Do not crowd scallops in the pan. The scallops should brown rather than steam. As scallops cook, remove from the pan and set aside on a warm plate, covered loosely.

When the chowder is cooked, remove 1 cup of the corn and potatoes and purée in a food processor. Return to stockpot. Add milk, stirring well, and heat over medium-low heat, 5 to 10 minutes. Do not allow the chowder to boil.

To serve, ladle a generous amount of chowder into soup bowls. Divide scallops between servings and garnish with chopped parsley and crumbled bacon.

French Onion Soup

SERVES 6

Beer is a natural ingredient in French onion soup. This tasty version from my recipe tester (and fellow beer lover) Jody Fijal is one of the best I've had.

> 3 tablespoons unsalted butter
> 3 tablespoons olive oil
> 8 cups sliced yellow onions
> $1/2$ teaspoon sugar
> 1 tablespoon all-purpose flour
> 3 cups beef broth
> 3 cups amber beer such as Old Detroit Amber Ale
>   or New Amsterdam Amber
> Salt and black pepper to taste
> $1 1/2$ to 2 cups shredded Swiss cheese
> 6 slices French bread

Melt butter and oil in a stockpot. Add onions and sugar, cover, and cook over medium heat, stirring occasionally until onions are tender, about 30 minutes. Uncover and add the flour, stirring to coat, and cook 5 minutes. Add the broth, beer, salt and pepper and cook, uncovered, for another 30 minutes.

Ladle soup into ovenproof soup bowls. Top with bread and $1/4$ to $1/3$ cup cheese. Place under broiler until cheese is golden brown. Serve immediately.

Beery Beans

SERVES 8

A new twist on Boston baked beans.

> 1 pound great Northern beans
> $1/4$ pound salt pork
> 1 teaspoon dry mustard
> $2 1/2$ cups stout such as Rogue Shakespeare Stout
>   or Saxer Three-Finger Jack Stout
> 1 teaspoon salt
> $1/2$ teaspoon freshly ground black pepper
> 1 yellow onion, sliced
> $3/4$ cup brown sugar

Rinse beans then add to 8 cups cold water. Bring to a boil then simmer 2 minutes and remove from heat. Cover and let stand for 1 hour. (Or cover beans with water and let soak overnight.)

Preheat oven to 300°. Cut salt pork in half and score one half. Thinly slice the remainder. Drain beans, reserving the liquid. In a 2-quart casserole, combine the beans, onion, sliced salt pork, dry mustard, stout, and salt and pepper. Pour sugar and bean liquid over. Top with scored salt pork.

Cover and bake, adding more liquid as needed, until done, 5 to 7 hours.

Portobello Mushroom and Roasted Garlic Risotto

SERVES 6

With the addition of a few hearty ingredients, risotto can be the star of a light-night supper. Portobello mushrooms are readily available, but you may substitute shiitakes or cremini.

1 head roasted garlic

2 tablespoons unsalted butter

2 tablespoons olive oil

8 ounces portobello mushrooms, stems removed
 and diced

2 large shallots, minced

$^1/_2$ cup lager beer such as Helles Gold Lager or
 Dock Street Illuminator

$5^1/_2$ cups chicken or beef stock

1 pound arborio rice

$^1/_2$ cup grated Parmesan cheese

$^1/_2$ cup chopped fresh parsley

1 teaspoon salt

1 teaspoon freshly ground black pepper

Remove pulp from garlic, mash in a small bowl, and set aside.

In a large saucepan over medium heat, melt butter with olive oil. Add mushrooms and shallots. Sauté, uncovered, until softened and just beginning to brown, 8 to 10 minutes.

Meanwhile, place the beer and stock in a medium saucepan and heat to medium.

Add rice to the sautéed vegetables, stirring to coat the rice grains. Add 1 cup of warm liquid, stir well, and reduce heat slightly to maintain a slow simmer. Add remaining liquid in 2 to 3 batches, stirring more in gently when liquid becomes absorbed. (A total of 20 to 30 minutes of stirring is required for a creamy consistency.) Stir in Parmesan, parsley, salt, and pepper, and serve immediately.

Cheddar and Chile Quick Bread

MAKES 1 LOAF

Beer combines with the cheese in this quick bread to produce a tender, moist loaf. It's particularly flavorful when served warm or lightly toasted.

2^1/$_2$ cups all-purpose flour

2 tablespoons sugar

1 tablespoon baking powder

1 tablespoon chile powder

1 teaspoon salt

1 teaspoon ground cumin

^{1}/$_2$ teaspoon baking soda

^{1}/$_2$ teaspoon cayenne pepper

1 cup grated sharp Cheddar cheese

^{1}/$_2$ cup grated pepper jack cheese

2 tablespoons grated Parmesan cheese

1 large egg

1^1/$_4$ cups amber beer such as McNeill's Fire House
      Amber Ale or Wild Goose Amber

1 roasted red pepper, seeded and diced

3 scallions, green part only, sliced thin

3 tablespoons canola oil

Preheat oven to 350°. Grease and flour a 9 x 5-inch loaf pan. In a large mixing bowl, which the first 8 ingredients. Add the three cheeses and stir to combine.

In a medium bowl, lightly whisk the egg. Add the beer, red pepper, scallions, and oil. Stir slightly to blend. Add the egg mixture to the dry ingredients and stir just until moistened.

Pour batter into loaf pan and bake 45 to 50 minutes or until top is deep golden brown, and a toothpick inserted in the center comes out clean. (Some cheese may stick to the toothpick.) Let break rest in pan 5 to 10 minutes. Carefully turn out onto cooling rack. Serve slightly warm or at room temperature.

Savory Spoonbread

SERVES 6

Beer serves as a leavener in this tender, light version of spoonbread—it's soft and soufflé-like, but won't fall when removed from the oven. Scoop out each serving with a large spoon and serve with a spicy tomato sauce, or as a side dish instead of rice or potatoes.

1 ¼ cups buttermilk

1 ¼ cups milk

½ cup wheat beer or pale ale such as Berkshire Brewing
      Steel Rail Extra Pale or Pete's Wicked Honey
      Wheat Ale

1 cup yellow or white cornmeal

3 large eggs, separated

½ cup thinly sliced scallions (green and white parts)

1 teaspoon salt

1 teaspoon Tabasco or other pepper sauce

2 teaspoons fresh thyme, minced

1 teaspoon black pepper

2 tablespoons grated Parmesan cheese

Preheat oven to 400°. Butter generously a 2-quart casserole or soufflé dish.

In a medium saucepan, place buttermilk, milk, and beer. Over medium heat, begin to slowly whisk in the cornmeal. (Mixture may look curdled.) Whisk continuously until smooth and thickened, 4 to 5 minutes.

Remove from heat. In a small bowl, whisk the egg yolks to blend. Slowly whisk in ¼ cup warm cornbread mixture, 2 tablespoons at a time, to gently warm the yolks without "cooking" them. Add the warmed yolk mixture back to the saucepan with the remaining thickened cornmeal mixture and stir to blend thoroughly. Stir in the remaining 6 ingredients. Remove pan from heat.

Meanwhile, beat the egg whites until stiff but not dry. Gently fold in the cornmeal-yolk mixture and blend thoroughly with a spatula. Pour into the buttered casserole and bake 40 minutes or until top is golden and spoonbread tests done.

Pork Tenderloin and Glazed Apples

SERVES 6

Pork tenderloin is a delicious cut of meat. Here, its flavor is enhanced by a tangy beer marinade, the sharpness of which is balanced by the sweetness of glazed apples.

3-pound pork tenderloin

1¼ cups plus ¼ cup wheat beer such as Pete's Wicked
    Honey Wheat Ale or Boulevard Wheat Beer

¼ cup tamari or soy sauce

2 tablespoons cider vinegar

2 tablespoons honey

1½ teaspoons mustard powder

1 teaspoon black pepper

½ teaspoon salt

4 sprigs fresh thyme, or 2 teaspoons dried

1 yellow onion, thinly sliced

3 large cloves garlic, thinly sliced

½ teaspoon ground allspice

4 firm tart apples such as Granny Smith

1 onion, thinly sliced

3 tablespoons unsalted butter

Pat the meat dry and set aside. Mix 1¼ cups beer with the next 10 ingredients in an 8 x 10-inch nonreactive pan or casserole dish. Add meat and turn to coat well. Cover and refrigerate for several hours or overnight.

Remove meat from marinade (reserving the marinade) and grill or broil 25 to 35 minutes or until internal temperature reads 135°, turn to brown all sides. Meanwhile, in a small saucepan, simmer reserved marinade uncovered, until reduced to 1 cup, 5 to 8 minutes. Strain.

Quarter the apples lengthwise and core. Slice into ½-inch wedges and toss with the onion, In a large nonstick skillet, melt the butter over medium high heat. Add apple mixture and remaining ¼ cup beer. Stir carefully and cook, turning the apples often to cook both sides evenly, until golden, and the moisture has reduced, 12 to 15 minutes. (You may need to cook the apples in 2 batches if your skillet is not large enough to make sure the apples don't steam and soften.)

Place the glazed applies around a serving plate. Slice the meat into ½-inch thick slices and place over apples. Drizzle reduced marinade over the meat and apples. Serve immediately.

Chorizo and Rice Bake

SERVES 6

Served with a green salad and cold beer, this is a satisfying one-dish meal. You can also cook this dish on the grill with a roasting pan suited for outdoor use (the cooking times are approximately the same for a grill kept at medium-high heat).

1 teaspoon cumin seed
1 teaspoon black peppercorns
1 dried red chile, such as a pasilla chile, stemmed
    and seeded (unless you like it spicy)
1 pound chorizo sausage
1 green bell pepper, coarsely chopped
1 red bell pepper, coarsely chopped
1 large yellow onion, coarsely chopped
3 cloves garlic, sliced thin
1 1/2 cups long-grain brown rice (see note)
4 fresh plum tomatoes, peeled, seeded, and diced
2 cups beef stock
2/3 cup pumpkin or amber ale such as Buffalo Bill's
    Pumpkin Ale
2 sprigs fresh rosemary, each about 4 inches long
Salt and black pepper to taste
1/2 cup chopped cilantro for garnish

In a small skillet over medium heat, toast the cumin seeds, peppercorns, and whole chile pepper until fragrant, about 30 seconds, shaking the pan constantly. Let cool, coarsely blend in a spice grinder, and set aside.

Remove the casing from the chorizo, split lengthwise, then cut into 1/2-inch slices. Preheat the oven to 375°. In a large roasting pan, combine the sausage with the peppers, onion, and garlic. Roast uncovered, stirring often, until evenly brown, about 25 minutes. If a lot of juice or grease has accumulated, remove all but 2 to 3 tablespoons. (This will depend on the meat and juiciness of the vegetables.)

Add rice and stir to coat with the juices. Add plum tomatoes, stock, beer, rosemary sprigs, and reserved spice blend. Stir well, cover tightly with foil, and bake about 45 minutes until rice is tender. Uncover and bake an additional 10 to 15 minutes to reduce the liquid. Taste and adjust seasoning with salt and pepper. Remove rosemary, and garnish generously with cilantro.

NOTE: You may substitute white rice, which will take less time to bake, about 30 minutes.

Harvest Beef Stew

SERVES 6 TO 8

This dish is easy to make: once all ingredients are prepared and assembled, it can be left to cook relatively unattended. The hearty dark stout tenderizes and sweetens the stew, and helps create a full, richly flavored gravy. Serve with garlic mashed potatoes or buttered noodles.

- $^1/_2$ ounce dried porcini mushrooms, plus 1 cup warm water for soaking
- $^1/_4$ pound bacon, chopped small
- $1^1/_2$ cups coarsely chopped yellow onions
- 1 leek, trimmed, split, and cut into $^1/_2$-inch lengths
- 3 large cloves garlic, peeled and left whole
- 3 carrots, peeled (split lengthwise if large), cut into $^1/_2$-inch rounds
- 3 small white turnips, peeled and quartered
- 2 parsnips, peeled (and split lengthwise if large), cut into $^1/_2$-inch lengths
- 2 teaspoons olive oil
- 3 pounds beef chuck, trimmed of fat, cut into $^1/_2$-inch cubes
- 1 teaspoon salt
- $^1/_2$ teaspoon black pepper
- $^1/_2$ cup flour
- 3 bay leaves
- 6 sprigs fresh thyme
- $^1/_2$ teaspoon Chinese five spice powder
- 3 cups beef broth
- 1 cup plus $^1/_2$ cup dark beer such as Adler Brau Oatmeal Stout or Grant's Imperial Stout
- Chopped parsley for garnish

Preheat oven to 325°.

In a small bowl, soak the mushrooms in warm water for 30 minutes, strain liquid and chop mushrooms coarsely. Set aside.

In a large, ovenproof casserole dish, brown the bacon and set aside. Add beef cubes (preferably in 3 to 4 batches), season with salt and pepper, and brown on all sides, about 3 to 5 minutes. Removed to a medium bowl.

Reduce heat to medium-low and sauté onions, leeks, and garlic until soft, about 5 minutes. Add remaining vegetables to casserole dish, cover and sweat about 10 minutes, stirring occasionally, until they being to soften.

Return browned beef and any collected juices to casserole dish with vegetables. Add the flour and stir to coat. Add the herbs, five spice powder, mushrooms, stock, and beer. Cover the casserole dish, place in oven, and bake for about $2^1/_2$ hours, or until meat and vegetables are tender.

To serve, remove bay leaves and thyme. Crumble the reserved bacon over the stew along with chopped parsley.

Lamb Shanks with Dried Fruits

SERVES 6

The shank portion of the leg meat has become the darling of chefs. It requires simple, slow cooking, which frees the cook to do other things. It is also conducive to a variety of spicy, hearty flavorings. Serve this dish with couscous to soak up the sauce.

6 lamb shanks (about $3/4$ to 1 pound each)

$1/4$ cup olive oil

1 tablespoon coriander seeds

2 teaspoons black peppercorns

1 tablespoon kosher salt

2 teaspoons sweet paprika

3 large yellow onions, peeled and cut in $1/2$-inch wedges

4 large carrots, peeled, cut in half, then quartered lengthwise

4 large cloves garlic, peeled

2 cinnamon sticks, each 3-inches long

Zest of 1 lemon

1 tablespoon dried oregano, crumbled

3 sprigs fresh rosemary

3 red serrano chiles, stemmed and seeded

4 cups chicken broth

1 cup pumpkin ale such as Buffalo Bill's Pumpkin Ale (see Note)

1 cup dried apricots

1 cup dried prunes

$1/2$ cup currants

$1/2$ cup golden raisins

Preheat oven to 350°. Pat dry meat and coat lamb with olive oil. In a small skillet over medium heat, toast the coriander seeds and peppercorns until fragrant, about 1 minute, shaking the pan constantly. Let cool. In a mortar and pestle or spice grinder, crush with the salt and paprika. Coat meat evenly with the spice rub.

In a large roasting pan, mix the onions, carrots, garlic, cinnamon, lemon zest, oregano, rosemary, and chile peppers.

Sear the meat, which can be done one of two ways: on a hot grill, turning until browned (not scorched) on all sides, or in a large skillet over medium high heat, turning to brown all sides. (You may need to do this in 2 to 3 batches, about 10 minutes per batch.) Place seared meat on top of vegetable mixture in the roasting pan. Pour chicken stock and beer over and around the meat. Cover and bake $1 1/2$ hours.

Uncover and baste meat well. Add the dried fruits and reduce heat to 300°. Bake, uncovered, 1 hours longer or until fork tender and the shanks are richly browned.

Remove the cinnamon sticks and rosemary stems from the sauce and serve immediately, with or without chiles.

Note: You can use an amber ale mixed with $1/4$ teaspoon pumpkin pie spices instead of the pumpkin ale.

Country-Style BBQ Ribs

SERVES 6

This cut of pork (from the meaty, rib-end of the pork loin) is especially suited to long oven-cooking and makes for a very tender and flavorful dish. It's similar in cut to the meat near the shoulder used for "pulled" barbecued pork in the South.

2 large yellow onions, sliced thin
4 to 5 pounds country-style ribs, trimmed of excess fat
1 teaspoon salt
$^1/_2$ teaspoon black pepper
$^1/_2$ teaspoon paprika
4 large bay leaves
$^3/_4$ cup amber beer such as Otter Creek Hickory Switch Smoked Amber Ale or Ashland Amber

BBQ Sauce:

1 tablespoon olive or corn oil
1 small yellow onion, diced
2 cloves garlic, minced
2 cups tomato sauce or 4 large tomatoes, peeled, seeded, and coarsely chopped
1 lemon, seeded and thinly sliced
$^1/_4$ cup amber lager such as Blue Hen Lager beer
2 tablespoons dark brown sugar
2 teaspoons Dijon mustard
2 teaspoons Worcestershire sauce
1 canned chipotle in adobo

Preheat oven to 375°. Place onions in bottom of large roasting pan that will hold them and the ribs comfortably. Pat meat dry. Mix salt, pepper, and paprika and use to season meat. Place meat over onions, and pour beer around meat. Cover tightly and bake $1^1/_2$ hours.

Meanwhile, make the sauce. Heat the oil in a medium saucepan. Sauté the onion and garlic in the oil until soft and golden, 2 to 3 minutes. Add remaining ingredients and simmer over medium-low heat, partially covered, until thickened, 30 to 35 minutes.

Remove the ribs from the oven, uncover, and discard the excess juices and grease that have accumulated, reserving $^3/_4$ cup. Mix reserved cooking juices with sauce and pour evenly over the ribs. Return the ribs to the oven and bake, uncovered, until tender and glazed, about 45 minutes, turning often and basting to keep the ribs evenly moist and coated with the sauce. Remove bay leaves and serve.

Fish Fillets en Papillote

SERVES 6

Baking fillets in parchment—a healthy alternative to broiling or sautéing—is a simple, savory way to prepare fish and impress guests with the presentation. Assemble the individual packets an hour or so before dinner, refrigerate, then bake as directed. The beer's dry, hoppy edge enhances the light flavor of the fish and its seasonings. Change the fish, vegetables, and herbs seasonally.

2 1/2 pounds thin fish fillets such as red snapper,
    sea bass, or sole
Zest of 2 lemons
6 scallions, cut in thin diagonal slices
3 carrots, julienned
5 ounces snowpeas, julienned
3 ounces fresh, young spinach leaves, cut into chiffonade
1/3 cup plus 2 tablespoons ale such as Pete's Wicked
    Honey Ale or Full Sail Amber Ale
1 tablespoons Dijon-style mustard
3 tablespoons clarified butter or olive oil
2 tablespoons minced fresh dill
1/2 teaspoon sea salt
1/2 teaspoon black pepper
6 large sheets of parchment paper (approximately 24 x 16
    inches or 6 inches larger on each side than the
    fillets)

Preheat oven to 400°. Pat dry the fillets and remove skin if necessary. In a medium bowl, toss the lemon zest with scallions, carrots, snowpeas, spinach, and 1/3 cup beer to moisten and blend evenly.

In a small bowl, whisk mustard with remaining 2 tablespoons beer, butter, dill, salt, and pepper. Taste and adjust seasoning.

To prepare the packets, place about 1/2 cup of the vegetable mixture off center on one sheet of parchment. Place a fish fillet on top. Distribute an additional 1/2 cup of vegetables over the fish, then drizzle or spoon about 2 teaspoons of the mustard sauce over the vegetables. Fold the parchment over the fish to form a packet or envelope. Fold the ends of the parchment in small folds, about 1/2-inch wide or less, several times, creasing each fold securely. Move to the next side and repeat folding technique. Fold remaining side, then place packed on large baking sheet. Prepare each packet in the same manner. If making ahead, refrigerate up to 2 hours.

Place packets on baking sheet and bake until parchments have puffed and are golden, 10 to 12 minutes. Do not overbake. To serve, place the packets on individual plates and carefully cut open.

Wild Rice Beer Stuffing

SERVES 6

This savory stuffing from the Capital Brewery in Wisconsin is splendid with chicken, Cornish game hens, and turkey. (It's also a tasty side dish when baked in a glass baking dish for 35 minutes at 350°.)

    1 yellow onion, chopped
    $1/2$ pound bulk pork sausage
    1 cup cooked wild rice
    8 ounces dry bread cubes or unseasoned croutons
    $1/2$ cup chopped walnuts
    $1/4$ teaspoon dried sage
    $1/8$ teaspoon dried rosemary
    $1/8$ teaspoon dried thyme
    $1/8$ teaspoon dried marjoram
    $1/8$ teaspoon dried basil
    $11/2$-ounce bottle Garten Brau Wild Rice Beer
        or other lager
    Black pepper to taste
    Salt to taste

Sauté onion and pork sausage until onions are transparent. Let cool. Mix all ingredients together and stuff 1 large chicken or 5 to 6 game hens.

Scotch Ale Marinade

MAKES $11/3$ CUPS

A delicious all-purpose marinade for meat, pork, or chicken.

    1 cup Scotch ale such as Samuel Adams
    3 cloves garlic, minced
    3 tablespoons minced ginger
    2 tablespoons brown sugar
    Juice of 1 lemon
    $1/4$ cup soy sauce
    1 tablespoon Worcestershire sauce
    $1/4$ cup freshly ground black pepper
    2 teaspoons cut dry lemon grass

Combine ingredients in bowl, mixing well. Store in refrigerator if not using immediately.

Jody's Whole Wheat Sunflower Bread

MAKES 3 LOAVES

Beer lovers will delight in this hearty, nutty bread with its yeasty flavor and suggestion of beer.

$3/4$ cup warm water

2 tablespoons active dry yeast

1 egg, beaten

$1/4$ cup melted butter

2 cups beers such as Stoudt's Gold or Samuel Adams
     Boston Lager

$1^1/2$ teaspoons salt

$1/2$ cup honey

4 cups whole wheat flour

4 cups all-purpose flour

$1/2$ cup cracked wheat

1 cup sunflower seeds

In a small bowl, combine the water and yeast and set aside 3 to 5 minutes. In a large bowl, combine the egg, butter, beer, salt, and honey, then add the yeast mixture. Add flours, cracked wheat, and sunflower seeds, and mix until the dough stops sticking to the sides of the bowl. Turn onto a floured board and knead 8 to 10 minutes. Place in a greased bowl, and allow to rise until doubled in bulk, approximately 2 hours. Punch down, divide into 3 greased loaf pans, and allow to rise again until doubled, approximately $1^1/2$ hours.

Preheat oven to 350°. Bake 40 to 50 minutes or until a toothpick inserted in the center comes out clean.

Caraway Biscuits

12 BISCUITS

When combined with beer, even the simplest of biscuits takes on a new personality and can be enjoyed with morning coffee, afternoon tea, or a hearty meal. The caraway seeds add a distinctive flavor and hark back to the days of Old England, when seed cake was popular and Shakespeare's Falstaff was offered "a pippin and a dish of caraways."

$1^3/_4$ cups all-purpose flour
$1/_4$ cup rye flour
1 tablespoon granulated sugar
2 tablespoons caraway seeds
$1^1/_2$ teaspoons baking powder
$1/_2$ teaspoon baking soda
1 teaspoon salt
$1/_2$ teaspoon freshly ground black pepper
6 tablespoons solid shortening, cut into small pieces
$2/_3$ cup amber or marzen beer such as New England
    Amber or Hubsch Marzen

Preheat oven to 425°. In a food processor fitted with a metal blade, pulse the dry ingredients to blend. Add shortening and pulse 4 to 5 times to cut in and make crumbly. With motor turned off, add beer, then pulse 6 to 8 times just to moisten. Do not overmix—mixture should be coarse and loose.

Turn out onto a lightly floured work surface. Knead about 8 times just until the mixture holds together; do not overwork. Gently pat or roll into a square about 8 x 6 x $1/_2$ inches. With a sharp knife cut into 12 squares. Place biscuits on an ungreased baking sheet $1/_2$-inch apart. Bake until tops are golden and biscuits have risen more than double, about 15 minutes.

Chocolate Spice Cake

MAKES 1 9-INCH LAYER CAKE

The spices and beer make a light but richly flavored layered cake that is satisfying with a light dusting of confectioners' sugar—or cover with a fluffy buttercream frosting or whipped cream and fresh raspberries.

2^1/$_4$ cups cake flour

^{1}/$_2$ cup cocoa powder

1^1/$_2$ teaspoons baking powder

1 teaspoon baking soda

1 teaspoon ground cinnamon

1 teaspoon ground allspice

^{1}/$_2$ teaspoon salt

^{3}/$_4$ cup unsalted butter at room temperature, cut into small pieces

1 cup packed light brown sugar

^{3}/$_4$ cup granulated sugar

2 teaspoons pure vanilla extract

2 large eggs, whisked lightly to break the yolks

^{2}/$_3$ cup beer such as Pete's Wicked Winter Brew or Spanish Peaks Honey Raspberry Ale

^{2}/$_3$ cup espresso or strong black coffee, cooled to room temperature

Confectioners' sugar

Preheat oven to 350°. Grease, flour, and line 2 (9-inch) round cake pans with parchment.

Sift together into a medium bowl the first seven ingredients. In the large bowl of an electric mixer, cream the butter, sugar, and vanilla on medium speed until smooth. Slowly add the eggs, beating thoroughly until smooth, scraping down the sides of the bowl as needed.

In a small bowl, mix the beer and coffee.

Reduce the speed of the mixer to medium-low, and add the flour alternately with the beer and coffee mixture, mixing in the flour before adding more liquid. End with the flour, scraping the sides and bottom of the bowl as needed to ensure all ingredients are well mixed. Do not overmix.

Divide the batter between the cake pans. Bake 25 to 30 minutes, or until a toothpick inserted in the center comes out clean. Cool in pans 5 minutes then turn out onto cooling racks. Let cool completely. To serve, dust with confectioners' sugar.

Spice Cake with Ginger and Beer

MAKES 1 CAKE

As the cool fall weather settles over New England, I particularly enjoy the warmth and fragrance of this spice cake as it bakes. The flavors of this autumn dessert are enhanced by the crystallized ginger and seasonal harvest beer brewed with pumpkin spices.

3 cups all-purpose flour
1 cup granulated sugar
$^1/_2$ cup packed light brown sugar
1 teaspoon baking soda
2 teaspoons baking powder
$^1/_2$ teaspoon salt
1 teaspoon cinnamon
1 teaspoon ground cloves
$^1/_4$ teaspoon nutmeg
$^1/_2$ cup golden raisins
$^1/_4$ cup diced crystallized ginger
$^1/_4$ cup diced dried apples
3 large eggs
$1^1/_2$ cups beer such as Buffalo Bill's Pumpkin Ale
$^3/_4$ cup safflower or canola oil

Grease and flour a 10-inch tube pan. Preheat oven to 350°. Combine the dry ingredients in the large bowl of an electric mixer, breaking up and distributing the brown sugar with your fingertips if needed. In a small bowl mix the raisins, ginger, and apples and set aside. In a separate bowl whisk the eggs slightly. Add beer and whisk to blend.

Add the oil to the dry ingredients in mixing bowl. Blend on medium-low speed until the mixture is crumbly, about 30 seconds. Add the egg and beer mixture and blend an additional 45 seconds. Scrape the bottom and sides of the bowl. Add the dried fruit mixture and blend on low speed about 15 seconds to distribute. Pour the batter into the prepared pan. Bake 1 hour and 15 minutes, or until a toothpick inserted in the center of the cake comes out clean. Cool in pan about 15 minutes then turn out onto a cooling rack.

Malt and Hop Varieties

Malts:

Made from barley kernels steeped in water and germinated for several days in special stone rooms before being lightly kiln-dried, malt gives beer a rounded sweetness. In the text, "L" refers to the Lovibond scale, which rates the color of the malt from light (1.5L) to dark (530L). Popular malt varieties include:

Black Patent: a roasted nearly black malt with a slightly burnt flavor. Used in stouts and porters, and in tiny quantities to lend a reddish tint to pale ales.

Caramel: copper-colored, with a nutty sweetness. Used to make amber and dark ales, and also lagers. Known in Britain as crystal malt.

Carapils: provides body and foam retention to ales.

Chocolate: a smooth, dark, rich, roasted malt with a chocolate-like flavor. Used in porters and dark ales.

Crystal: see caramel malt.

Halcyon Pale Ale: an English malt, still relatively rare in the U.S. Used in Indian Pale Ales.

Munich: a high-kilned lager malt that is rich, aromatic, and suggestive of caramel.

Pale: a light golden malt that has a rounded, smooth feel and rich, earthy, sometimes sweet undertones. The base malt of most beers.

Roasted Barley: unmalted barley that is roasted raw until it is dark brown. Preferred over black patent because it provides a smoother, coffee-like, somewhat smoky, roasted flavor without the bitterness.

Six-row Barley: a pale malt named after the barley from which it is made (with six rows of grain on each ear). From the Northwest and Midwest.

Two-row Barley: pale malt made from barley with two rows of grain on each ear. Grown in the Northwest, Canada, and Northern Europe.

Two-row English Pilsner: an English malt used to make pilsner lagers.

Two-row English Pipkin: an English malt, relatively rare in the U.S. Used in Indian Pale Ales.

Victory Malt: a toasted, nutty malt used in nut brown ales, porters, and other ales.

Vienna: a high-kilned lager malt with a full-bodied malt character.

Wheat: used in wheat beers, with a soft sweetness.

Hops:

In vineyards throughout the world, hundreds of hop varieties are cultivated. (They grow on climbing, twisting stems called bines.) Hops added at the beginning of the boiling stage led a dry, bitter flavor, while hops added later create an herbal bouquet and fresh "hoppy" finish. Popular varieties include:

Brewers Gold: a strong bittering hop from the U.S. and U.K. used in stouts and other ales.

Bullion: a good, all-purpose bittering hop from the U.S. and U.K.

Cascade: a bittering, finishing, and aroma hop with a citrus-like (grapefruit) and floral aroma, from the U.S.

Centennial: an American hop similar to Cascade, but stronger, with a pronounced citrus quality.

Challenger: a rare British hop.

Chinook: an American bittering hop developed in the last decade.

Clusters: a traditional American bittering hop—some claim it has poor flavor and prefer Cascade or Galena

Columbia: a rare American hop.

Eroica: a U.S. bittering hop used in dark ales and stouts.

Fuggles: an aromatic British hop developed at the turn of the century, with a mild floral quality, used in ales and dark lagers (recognizable in Guinness). Also grown in the U.S.

Galena: a popular bittering hop that was developed in the U.S.

Goldings: a traditional 18th-century British bittering and aroma hop used in ales, now also grown in the U.S. and Canada.

Hallertauer: a delicate hop, with a distinct spicy aroma. Grown in the U.S. and Germany (in the region north of Munich). Used in many lagers.

Hallertauer Hersbrucker: a traditional aromatic hop from Germany, with a terrific spicy aroma.

Hallertauer Mittelfrueh: a traditional German lagering hop that is herbal and aromatic. Used for German-style lagers.

Kent Goldings: similar to Goldings, this traditional bittering, finishing, and aroma hop for ales has a spicy earthy pungency. Grown in the U.K.

Mt. Hood: a good aromatic American hop developed from a strain of German Hallertauer.

Northern Brewer: a pleasing European bittering hop for dark ales, pale ales, and dark lagers. Grown in the U.S.

Nugget: a new bittering hop from the U.S. with a good aroma.

Olympic: a rare American hop.

Perle: bred as an American replacement for Hallertauer, this is a good traditional bittering and aroma hop for lagers (except pilsners). Found in the Northwest.

Saaz: from the Zatec area in western Bohemia (the Czech Republic), this is a prized pilsner aromatic hop that is delicate, floral, and spicy.

Saxon: a rare British hop.

Spalt: a noble German hop used for bittering and aroma in many lagers.

Stickelbract: a bitter hop from New Zealand and Australia.

Tettnanger: a terrific spicy hop from Germany, now also grown in the U.S. Suitable for all lagers.

Viking: a rare British hop.

Willamette: an American version of Fuggles. Good as an aromatic hop in either ales or lagers.

Resources

This section covers periodicals, organizations, sources, and festivals.

Periodicals:

Ale Street News
P.O. Box 1125
Maywood NJ 07607
(800) 351-ALES

All About Beer
1627 Marion Avenue
Durham, NC 27705
(800) 977-BEER

American Brewer Magazine
P.O. Box 510
Hayward, CA 94543
(510) 538-9500

American Breweriana Journal
P.O. Box 11157
Pueblo, CO 81001
(719) 544-9267

Barley Corn Magazine
P.O. Box 2328
Falls Church, VA 22042
(703) 573-8970

Celebrator Beer News
P.O. Box 375
Hayward, CA 94543
(510) 670-0121

The Erickson Report
P.O. Box 1895
Sonoma, CA 95476
e-mail: JERedBrick@aol.com

Head's Up Magazine
150 Paularino Avenue
Costa Mesa, CA 92626
(800) 441-BEER

Juice Magazine
P.O. Box 9068
Berkeley, CA 94709
(510) 841-6655

Malt Advocate
3416 Oak Hill Road
Emmaus, PA 18049
(610) 967-1083

Midwest Beer Notes
339 6th Avenue
Clayton, WI 54004
(715) 948-2990

The New Brewer
P.O. Box 1679
Boulder, CO 80306
(303) 447-0816

Northwest Brew News
22833 Bothell-Everett Highway
Suite 1139
Bothell, WA 98021
(206) 742-5327

ON TAP: The Newsletter
P.O. Box 71
Clemson, SC 29633
(803) 654-3360

Pint Post
12345 Lake City Way NE
Seattle, WA 98125
(206) 527-7331

Southern Draft News
702 Sailfish Road
Winter Springs, FL 32708
e-mail: http://RealBeer.com
    /sodraft

Southwest Brewing News
11405 Evening Star Drive
Austin, TX 78739

The Spirits Journal
421-13 Route 59
Monsey, NY 10952

World Beer Review
P.O. Box 71
Clemson, SC 29633

Yankee Brew News
P.O. Box 8053, JFK Station
Boston, MA 02114
(617) 461-5963

*Zymurgy: Journal of the American
    Homebrewers Association*
P.O. Box 1679
Boulder, CO 80306-1679
(303) 447-0816

Organizations:

American Brewers' Guild
2110 Regis Drive #B
Davis, CA 95616
(916) 753-0497

American Malting Barley
    Association
735 North Water Street
Milwaukee, WI 53202
(414) 272-4640

American Society of Brewing
  Chemists
3340 Pilot Knob Road
St. Paul, MN 55121
(612) 454-7250

Association of Brewers
P.O. Box 1679
Boulder, CO 80306
(303) 447-0816

Beer Can Collectors of America
747 Merus Court
Fenton, MO 63026
(314) 343-6486

Brewer's Association of America
P.O. Box 876
Belmar, NJ 07719
(908) 280-9153

Brewer's Guild
8 Ely Place
Holborn Circus
London EC1N6SD
England

Brewer's Society
41 Portman Square
London W1HOBV
England
(011) 44-71-486-4831

Campaign for Real Ale Limited
34 Alma Road
St. Albans AL13BW
England

Hop Growers of America
7 West Meade Avenue
Yakima, WA 98909
(509) 248-7043

Hop Research Council
P.O. Box 1441
Yakima, WA 98907
(509) 575-5411

Institute for Brewing Studies
P.O. Box 1679
Boulder, CO 80306
(303) 447-0816

Master Brewer's Association
  of the Americas
2421 North Mayfair Road
Wauwatosa, WI 53226
(414) 774-8558

Microbrew Appreciation Society
12345 Lake City Way NE
Seattle, WA 98125
(206) 527-7331

MidAtlantic Association of
  Small Brewers
1327 North Vernon Street
Arlington, VA 22201
(703) 527-1441

Museum of Beverage
  Containers
1055 Ridgecrest Drive
Gatlinburg, TN 37072
(615) 859-5236

The Beer Institute
1225 Eye Street NW
Washington, DC 20005

Also check out the terrific beer
forum on Compuserve.

Sources:

Ale in the Mail
(800) 5-SEND-AL

American Beer Club
6399 142nd Avenue North,
#117
Clearwater, FL 34620
(800) 953-BEER

Beer Across America
150 Hilltop Avenue
Barrington, IL 60011
(800) 854-BEER

Great American Beer Club
480C Scotland Road
Lakemoor, IL 60050

Microbrew Express
2246 Calle del Mundo
Santa Clara, CA 95054
(800) 671-BREW

The Brew Tour
P.O. Box 471
Oregon City, OR 97045
(800) 660-8687

Festivals:

Please note that festivals change from year to year, and are often organized by volunteers who list their work phone. So if you call about a festival and are confused when you get General Mills headquarters and no one has heard of the Yeast Festival, fear not: simply call the local chamber of commerce as an alternate.

February:

Great Alaskan Winter Brew and
    Barley Wine Festival
Anchorage, AK
(907) 276-BEER

Northwest Microbrew
    Exposition
Eugene, OR
(541) 485-3907

March:

American Institute of Wine and
    Food Beer & Food Fest
New York, NY
(212) 447-0456

Berkshire County Brewer's
    Festival
Pittsfield, MA
(413) 499-3333 or e-mail:
steph@live105wbec.com

Great Arizona Beer Festival
Phoenix, AZ
(602) 780-3523 or e-mail:
forbes@primenet.com

International Beer Festival
Peoria, IL
(309) 682-2500

Oldenberg Beer Camp
Fort Mitchell, KY
(606) 341-7223

April:

Bakersfield Festival of Beers
Bakersfield, CA
(805) 631-7363 or e-mail:
garrison@acni.com

California Beer Festival
San Diego, CA
(619) 225-9813

Chicago Beer Society All Ameri-
    can Beer Tasting
Chicago, IL
(708) 973-0240

Seattle Brew Fest
Seattle, WA
(206) 365-5812

Spring Beer Fest
Portland, OR
503-246-4503 or e-mail:
springfest@jhw.com

May:

Boston Brewers Festival
Boston, MA
(617) 547-2233 or 800-565-
4BRE

California Festival of Beers
San Luis Obispo, CA
(805) 544-2266

Great Alaska Craftbeer and
    Homebrew Festival
Haines, AK
(800) 542-6363

Hilton Head International Beer
    Festival
Hilton Head Island, SC
(800) 689-3440

International Beer Festival
San Francisco, CA
(415) 346-6971 or e-mail:
dave.champine@schwab.com

Midwest International Beer
    Exposition
Chicago, IL
(847) 678-0071

Oregon Homebrew Competi-
    tion and Festival
Albany, OR
(541) 926-2286 or e-mail:
struble@ucs.orst.edu

Rawley's Breweriana Extrava-
    ganza
Sunnyvale, CA
(408) 245-6109

Yeast Feast
Williamsport, PA
(717) 398-7383

June:

Brew-Ha-Ha Beer Tasting
Festival
Half Moon Bay, CA
(415) 726-2729

California Brewmasters Classic
San Francisco, CA
(408) 375-7275

Colorado Brewers Festival
Fort Collins, CO
(303) 498-9070 or
(800) 274-FORT

Great Eastern Microbrewers
Festival
Adamstown, PA
(717) 484-4386

Great New England Brewer's
Festival
Northampton, MA
(413) 586-1850 or e-mail:
joe@crocker.com

Great Hawaiian Beer Festival &
Competition
Honolulu, HI
(808) 259-6884 or e-mail:
brew@lava.net

International Brewmaster's
Festival
Vancouver, BC
Canada
(604) 732-3377

Wichita Festival of Beers
Wichita, KS
(316) 838-7707 ext. 1222

July:

California Small Brewers
Festival
Mountain View, CA
(415) 965-2739

KQED Beer and Food Festival
San Francisco, CA
(415) 553-2200

Oregon Brewers Festival
Portland, OR
(503) 778-5917 or
(503) 226-7623

Small Brewer's Festival of
California
Mountain View, CA
(800) 965-BEER

August:

Great British Beer Festival
London
(011) 44-172-786-7201

Great Rocky Mountain Beer
Festival
Copper Mountain, CO
(303) 968-2318

Boulder Brewers' Festival
Boulder, CO
(303) 444-8448

Southern Brewers Festival
Chattanooga, TN
(800) 737-2311 or e-mail:
bhama@aol.com

September

Great Eastern Micro Festival
Adamstown, PA
(717) 484-4387

Great Northwest Microbrewery
Invitational
Seattle, WA
(206) 232-2982

Mid-Atlantic Beer & Food
Festival
Washington, DC
(703) 527-1441

New York Beer Festival
Brooklyn, NY
(718) 855-7882

Oldenberg Beer Camp
Fort Mitchell, KY
(606) 341-7223

Steamboat Fall Foliage Festival
& BrewFest
Streamboat Springs, CO
(970) 879-0880 or e-mail:
skramer@steamboat-
chamber.com

Vermont Brewers Festival
Burlington, VT
(800) 864-5927

October:

Calistoga Beer & Sausage
Festival
Calistoga, CA
(707) 942-6333 or e-mail:
ca94515@aol.com

Great American Beer Festival
Denver, CO
(303) 447-0816

Harpoon Octoberfest
Boston, MA
(617) 455-1935

Microbrewer's Octoberfest
Chicago, IL
(312) 836-4338

Newport Microbrew Festival
Newport, OR
(503) 265-3188 or
(503) 265-4649

November:

Chicago Beer Society International Beer Tasting
Chicago, IL
(708) 973-0240

Great Canadian Beer Festival
Victoria, BC
Canada
(604) 595-7729 or e-mail:
jrowling@galaxy.gov.bc.ca

Great Belgium Beer Festival
Antwerp, Belgium
(011) 32-16-651-093
or e-mail:
PCrombecq@AntwerpCity.be

Bibliography

Finch, Christopher and W. Scott Griffiths. *America's Best Beers*. Little Brown, 1994.

Jackson, Michael. *The New World Guide to Beer*. Courage, 1988.

Johnson, Steve. *On Tap Guide to North American Brewpubs*. WBR Publishing, 1993.

Klein, Bob. *The Beer Lover's Rating Guide*. Workman, 1995.

LaFrance, Pete. *Beer Basics*. Wiley, 1995.

Nachel, Marty. *Beer Across America*. Storey Publishing, 1995.

Ward, Philip. *Home Brew*. Lyons & Burford, 1995.

If you like the cover of this book, you'll love Jennifer's *American Microbrewery Beers* and *The Classic Beer Guide* posters, available from Celestial Arts, 800-841-BOOK.

For more information about books, posters, sauces, and products by Jennifer Trainer Thompson, contact JT[2] Productions, 560 North Hoosac Road, Williamstown, MA 01267 or e-mail Jennifer at 75050.1417@compuserv.com.

"For we could not now take time for further search (to land our ship) our victuals being much spent, especially our Beers."

—LOG OF THE MAYFLOWER

Index

Index

Index